January 2004.

Thank you very mu
your hospitality. Ou
Experience will alw
remembered - even when we
resemble the ladies on the cover!

Good Health always.

Lois.

MOMENTS

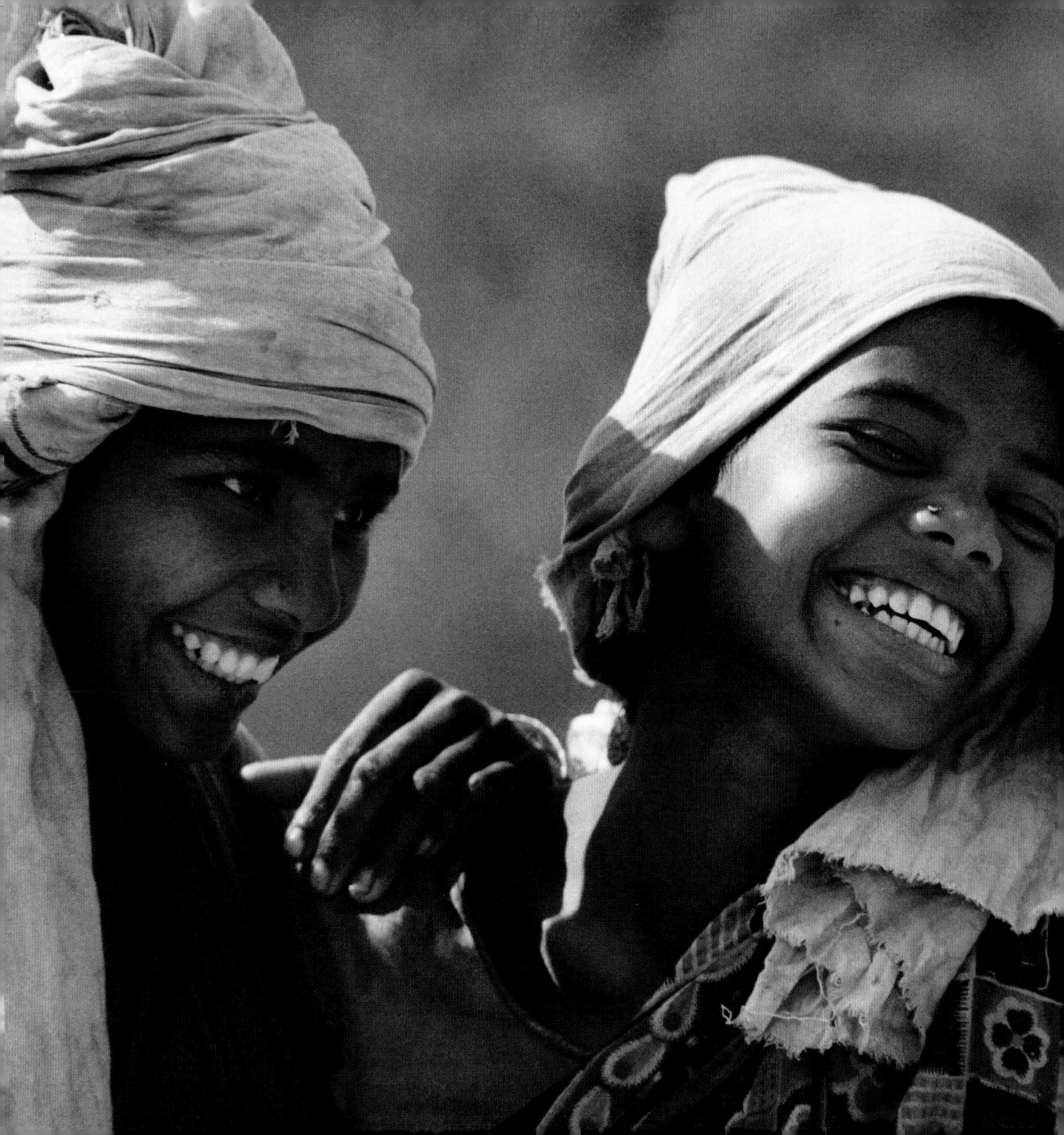

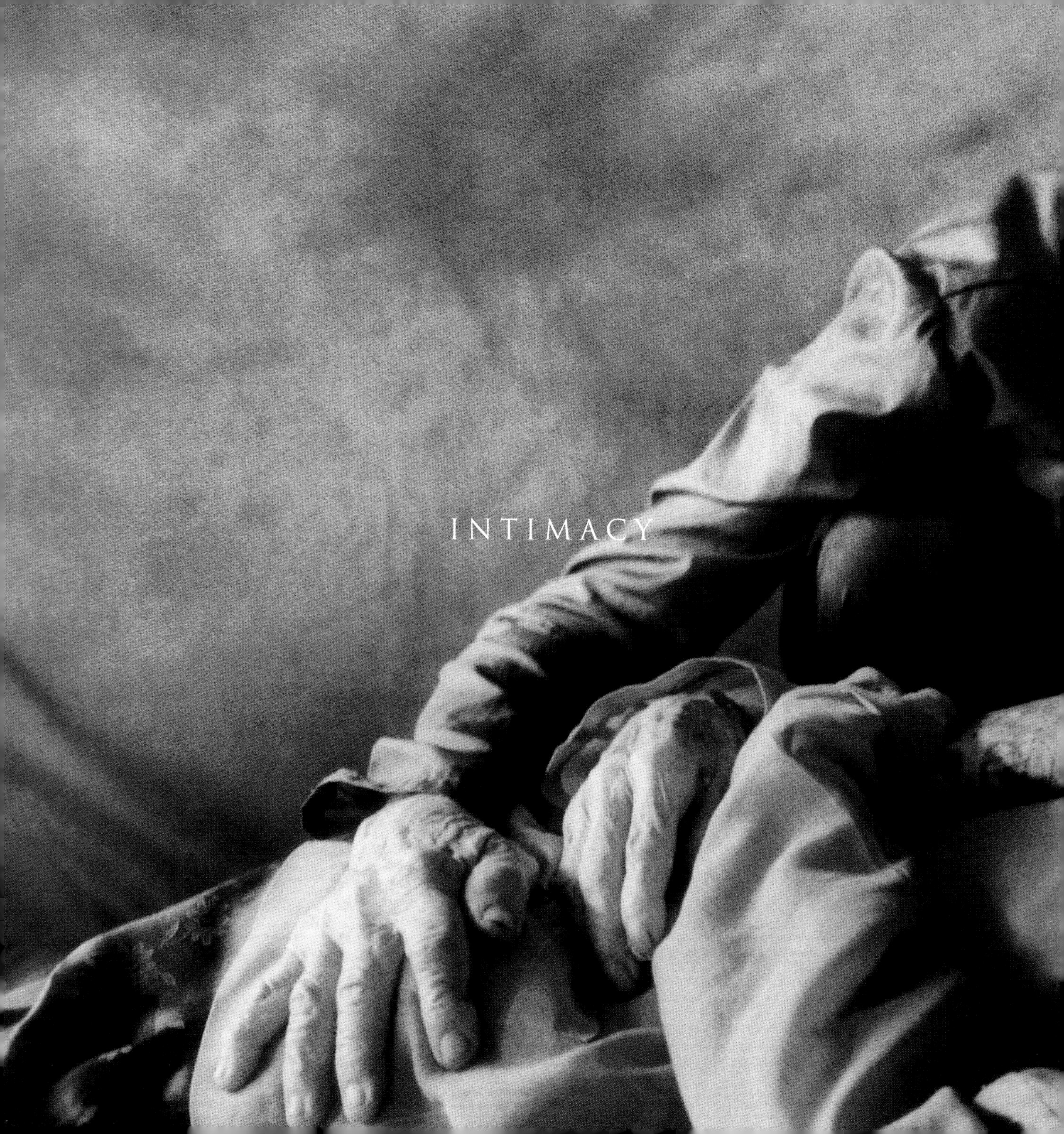

INTIMACY

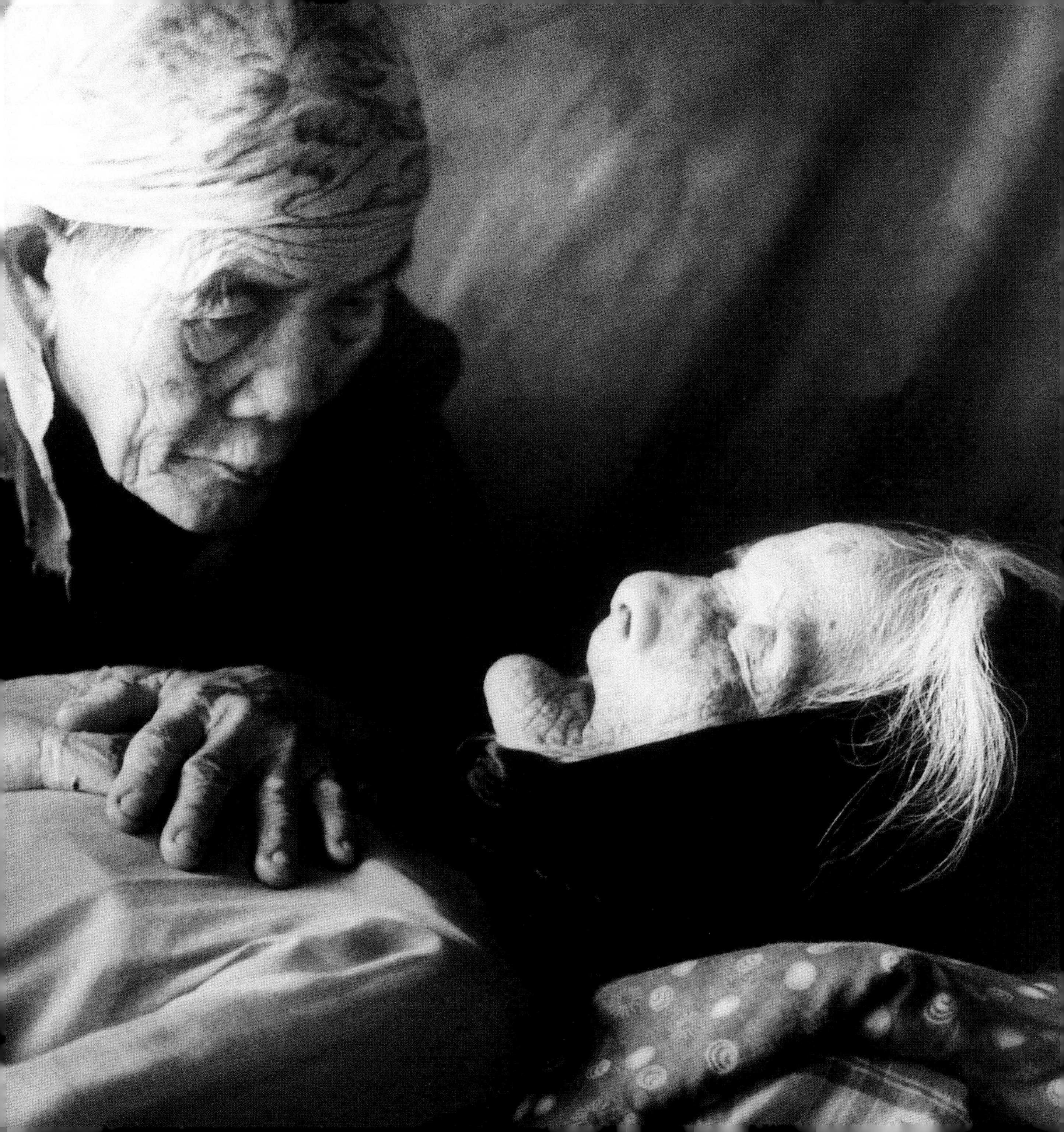

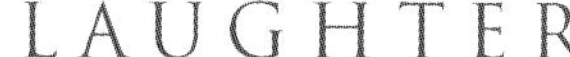
LAUGHTER

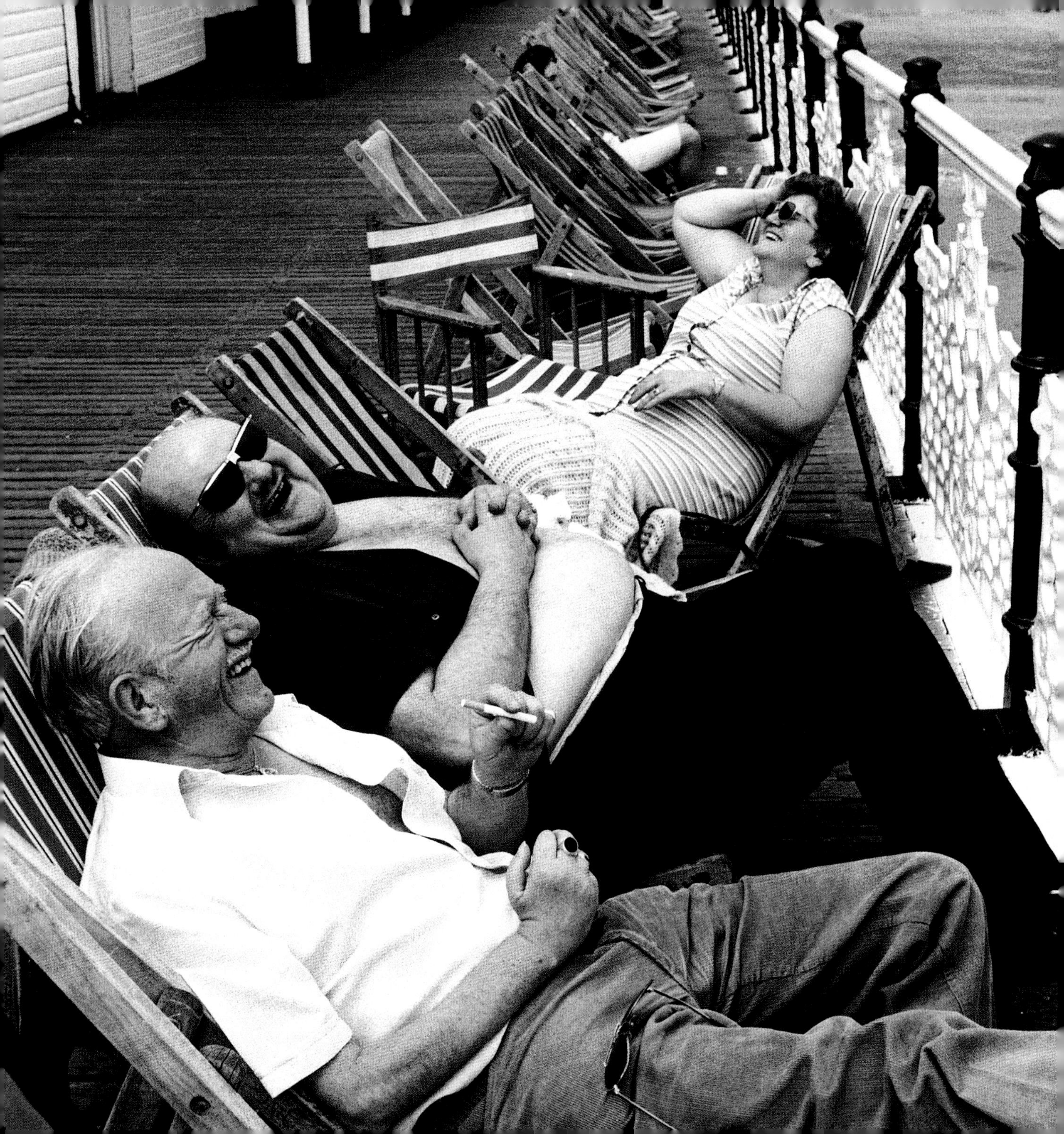

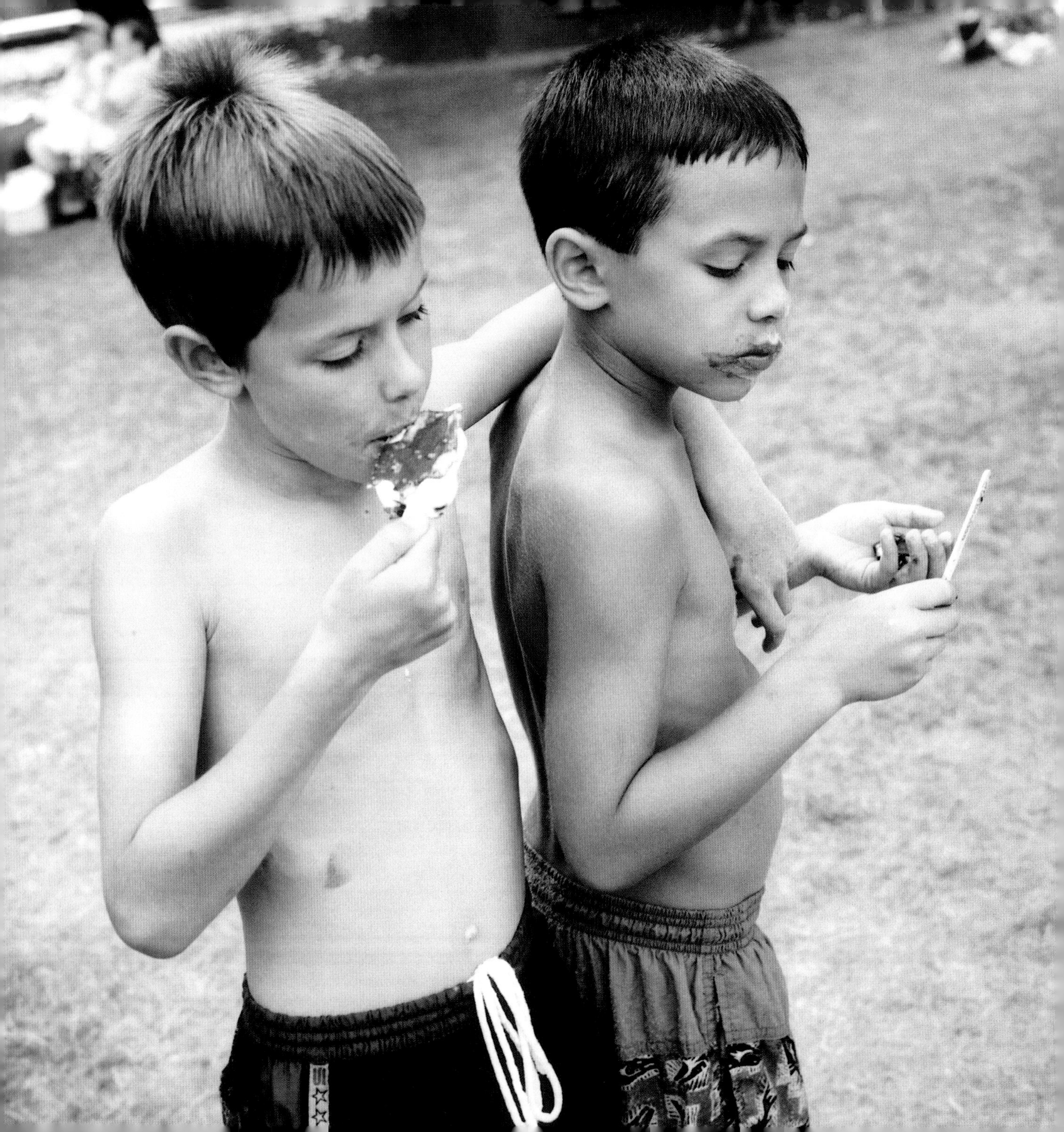

KINSHIP

GOOD FRIENDS

MOMENTS INTIMACY LAUGHTER KINSHIP

HODDER

M·I·L·K

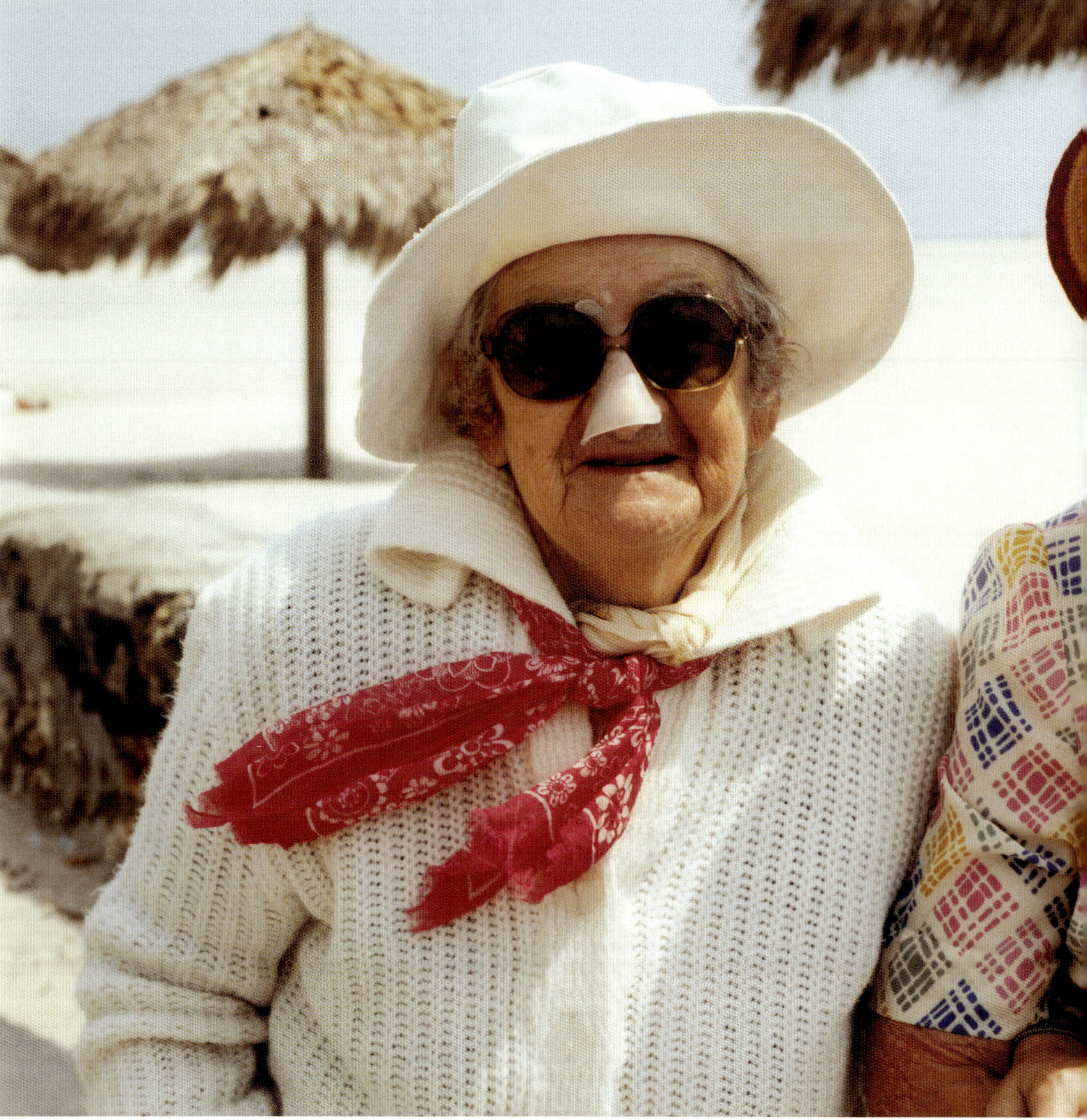

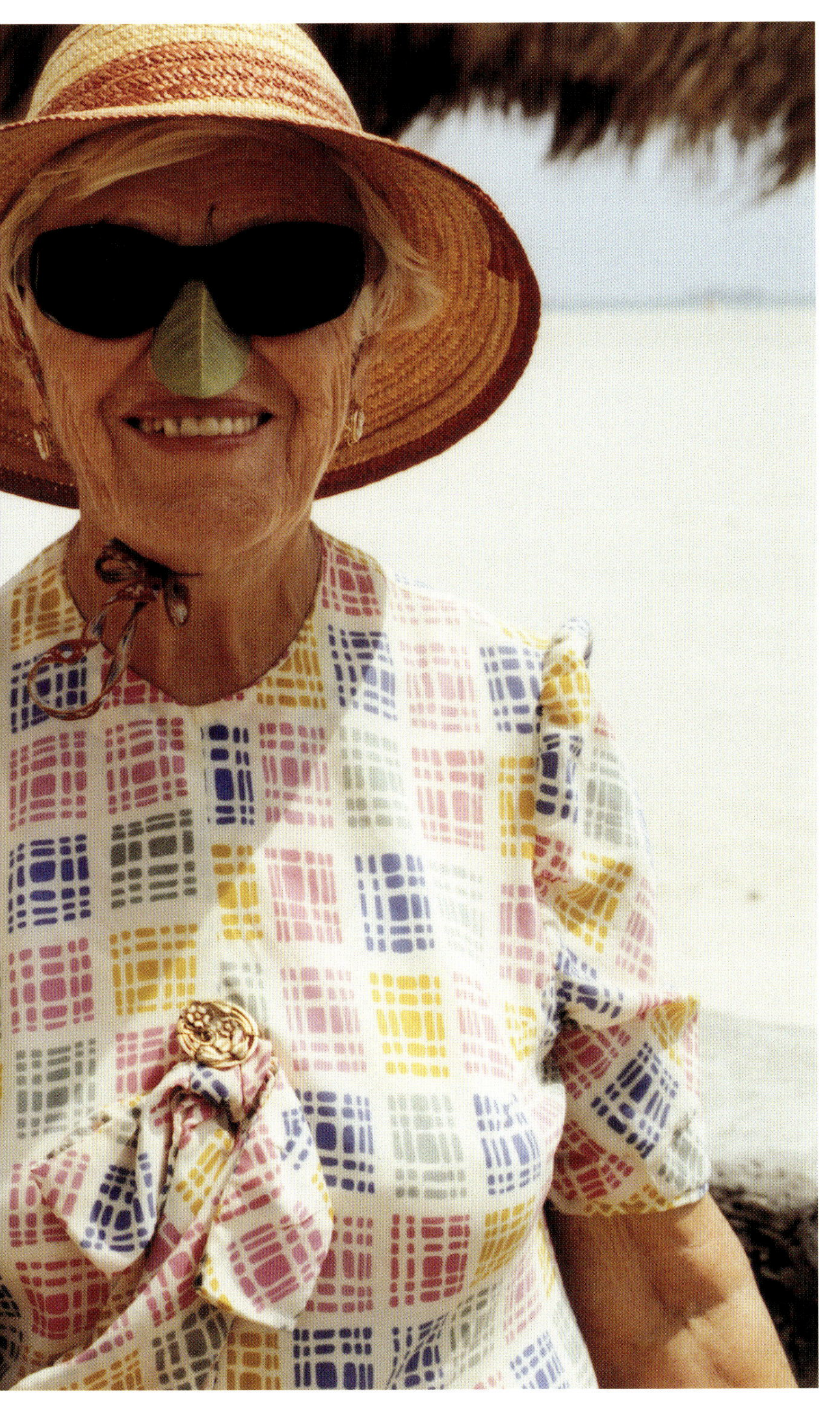

Our hope is that you will look
through this book
and recognize the people in it –
their moments are our moments.

These images speak to us all with clarity,

universality... and joy.

The images in this book were selected from the winners of an international photographic competition that was staged to launch a project called "M.I.L.K.".

The competition involved 17,000 photographers from 164 countries and was conceived to find images from around the world that celebrate humanity and its relationships. Over 40,000 photographs were submitted for judging – some in lovingly stitched cloth packages, others alongside warm and heartfelt messages of support and encouragement – unforgettable images of human life from its first fragile moments to its last.

M.I.L.K. is an acronym. The expanded version – Moments of Intimacy, Laughter and Kinship – neatly describes that which we set out to find at the beginning of this project. The truth, however, is that these words don't begin to describe the pleasure and satisfaction we, the M.I.L.K. team, found along the way.

And so, the images are here for you to enjoy. My hope is that you will look through this book and recognise the people in it – their moments are our moments. The instants of their lives captured here are universal. These images speak to us all with clarity, universality and to use that elusive and neglected word – joy.

These images, and this book, are a celebration of what it is to be part of a family, to share the gift of friendship, and more than anything else, to be loved. I hope that you and your friends will enjoy them because these moments of intimacy, laughter and kinship belong to you.

Geoff Blackwell M.I.L.K.

A friend is, as it were, a second self.

[CICERO]

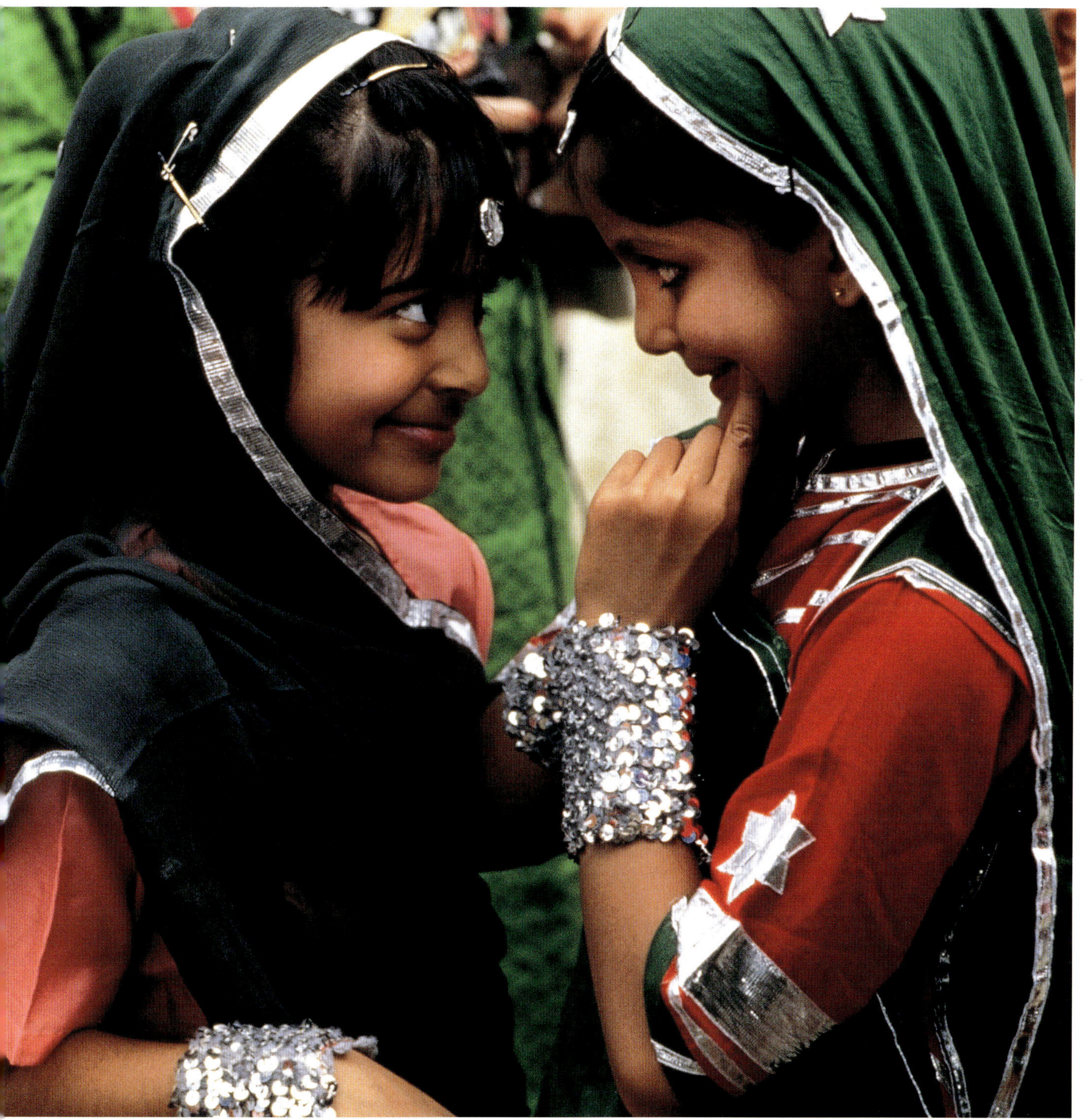

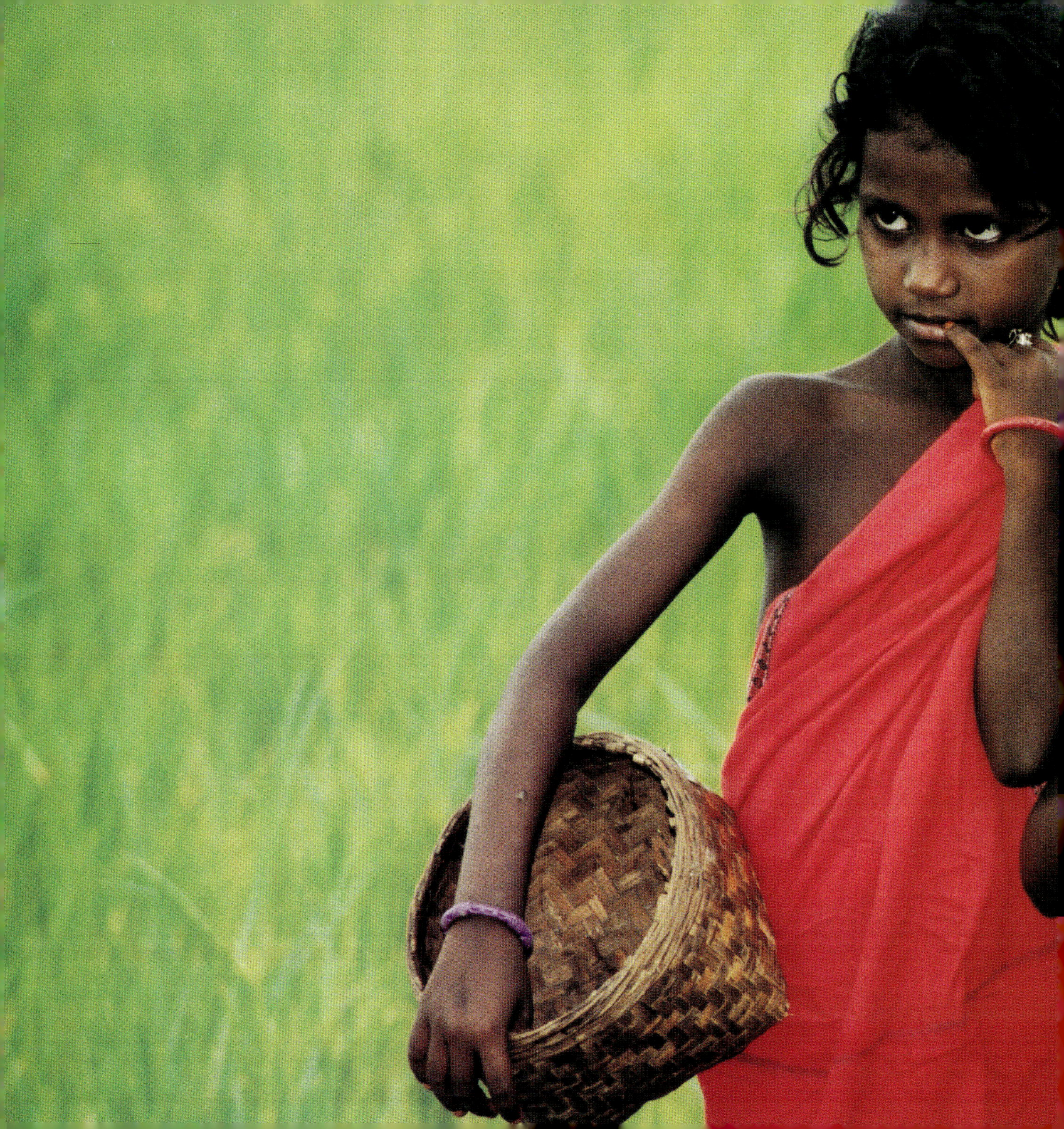

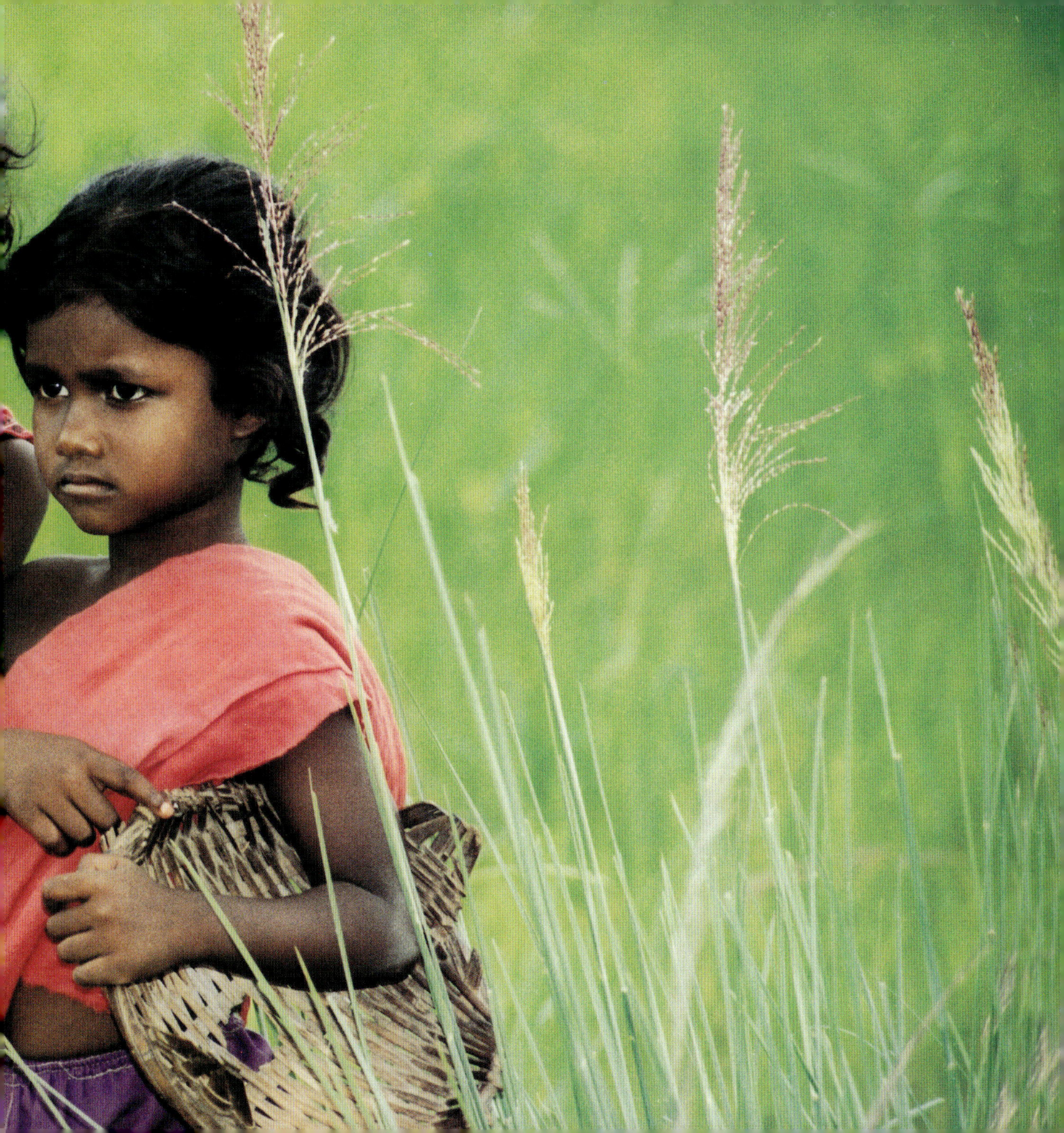

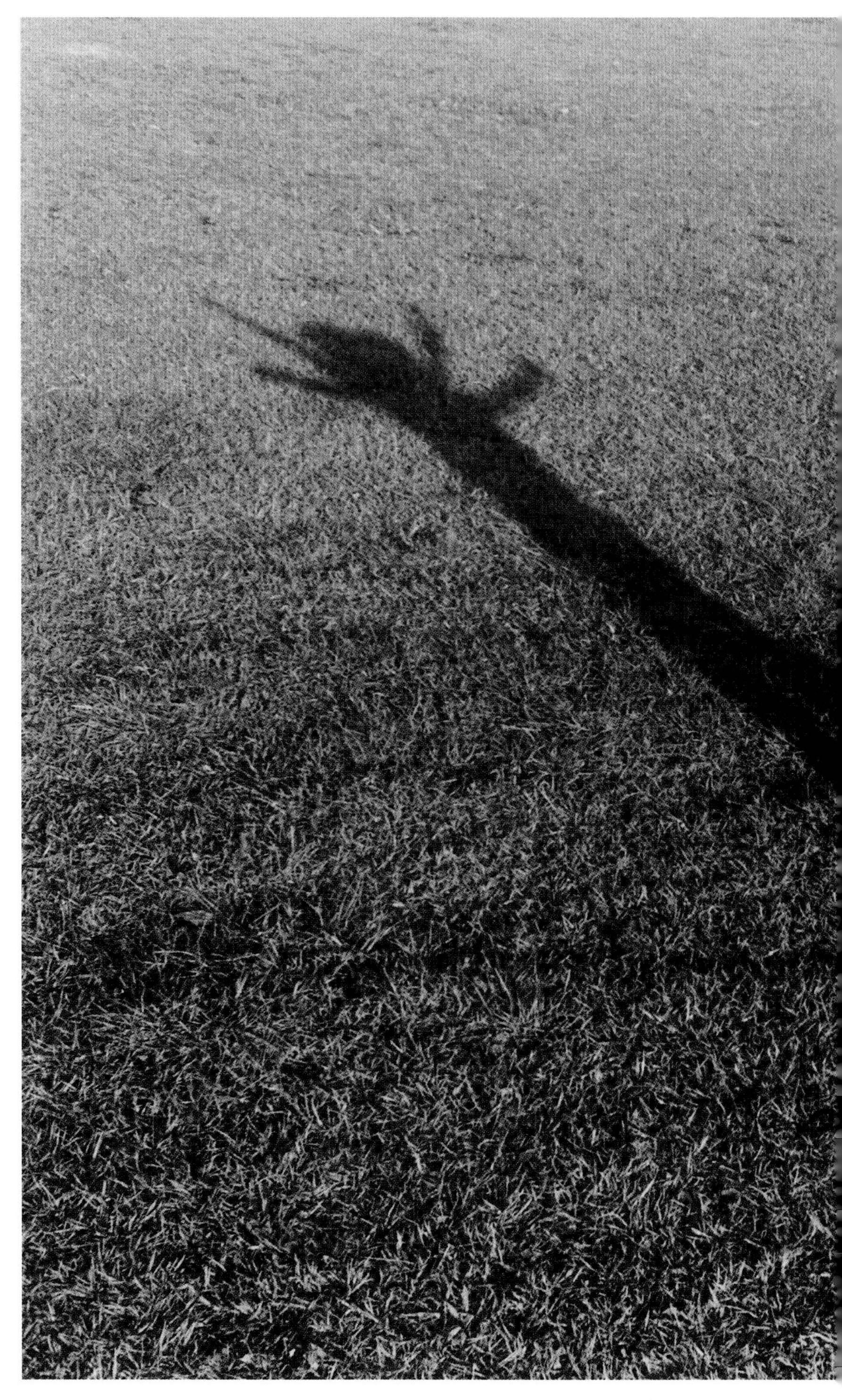

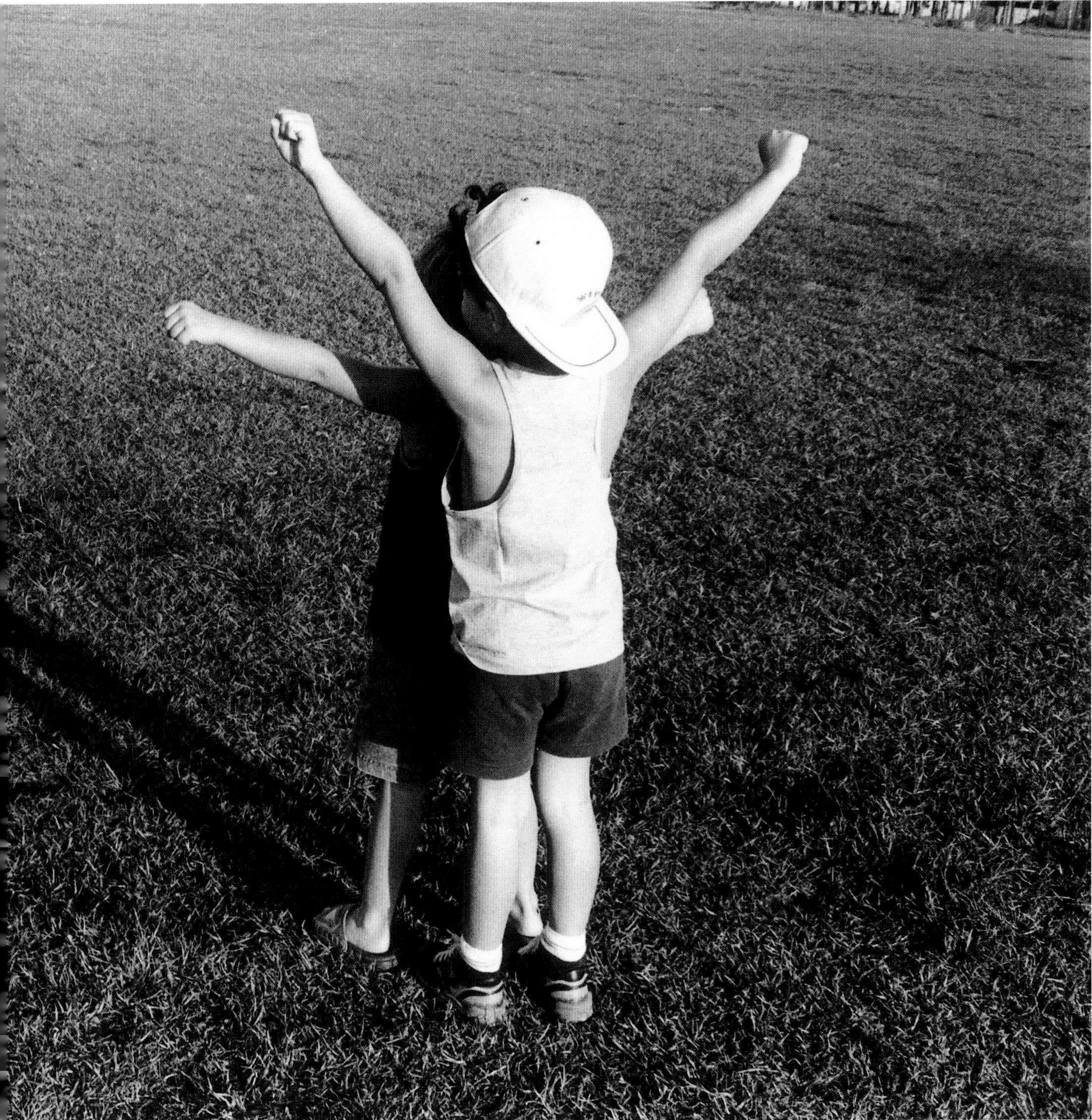

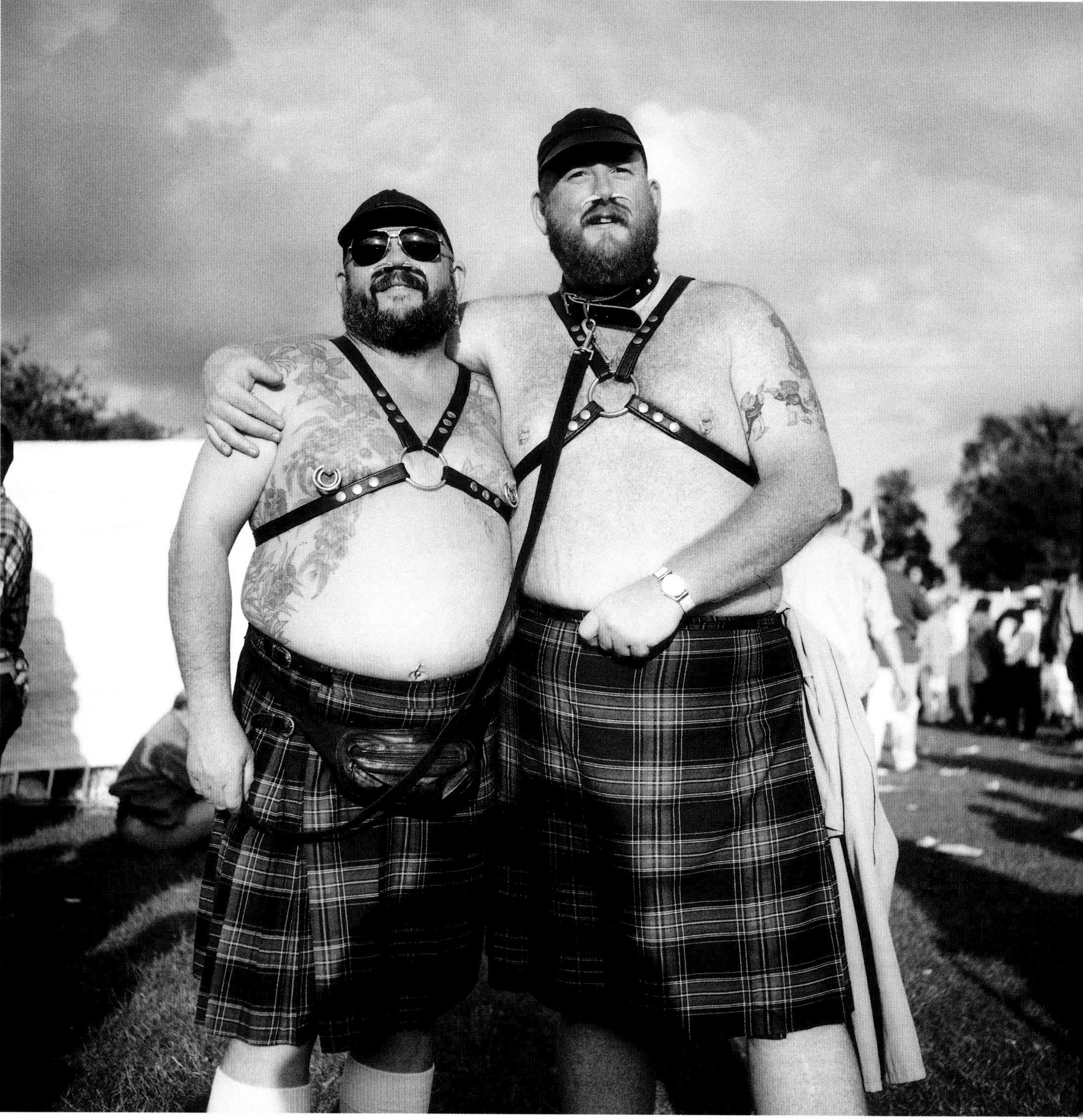

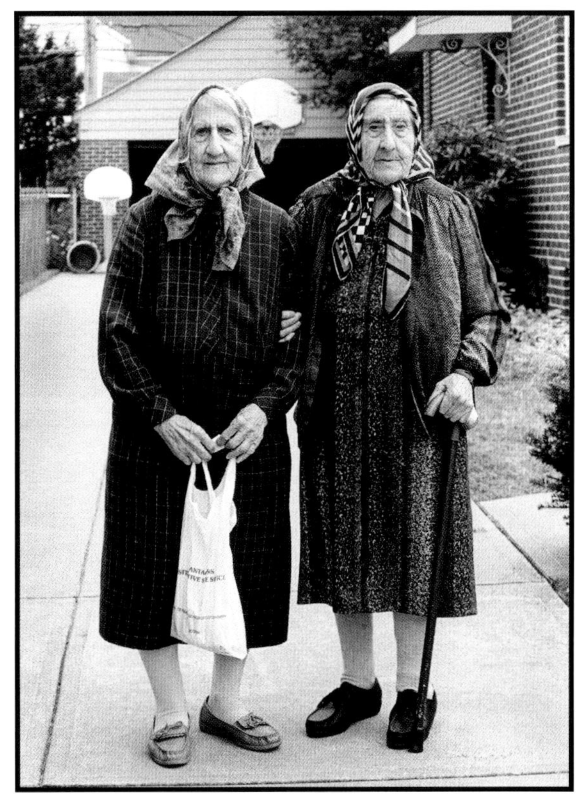

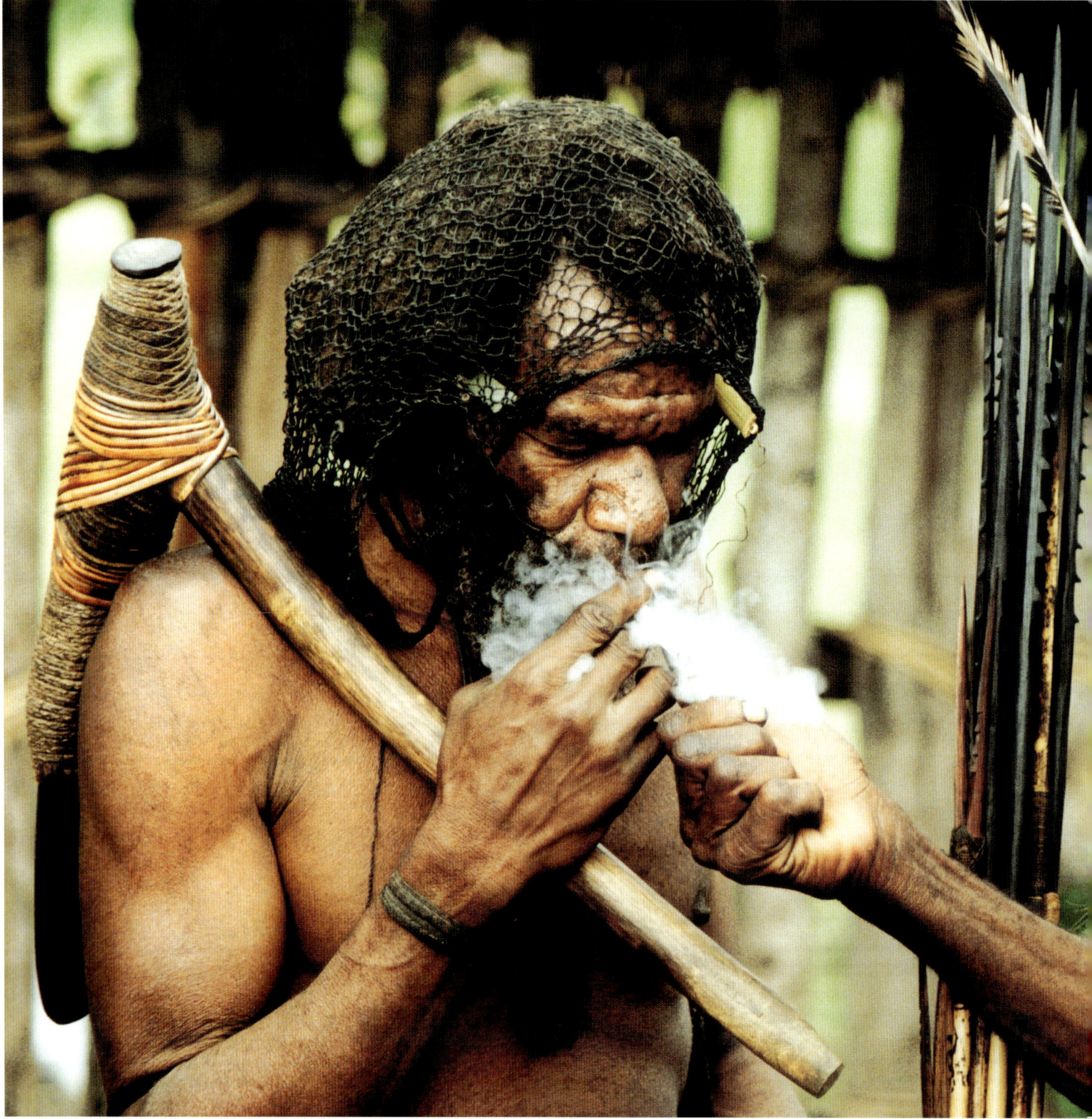

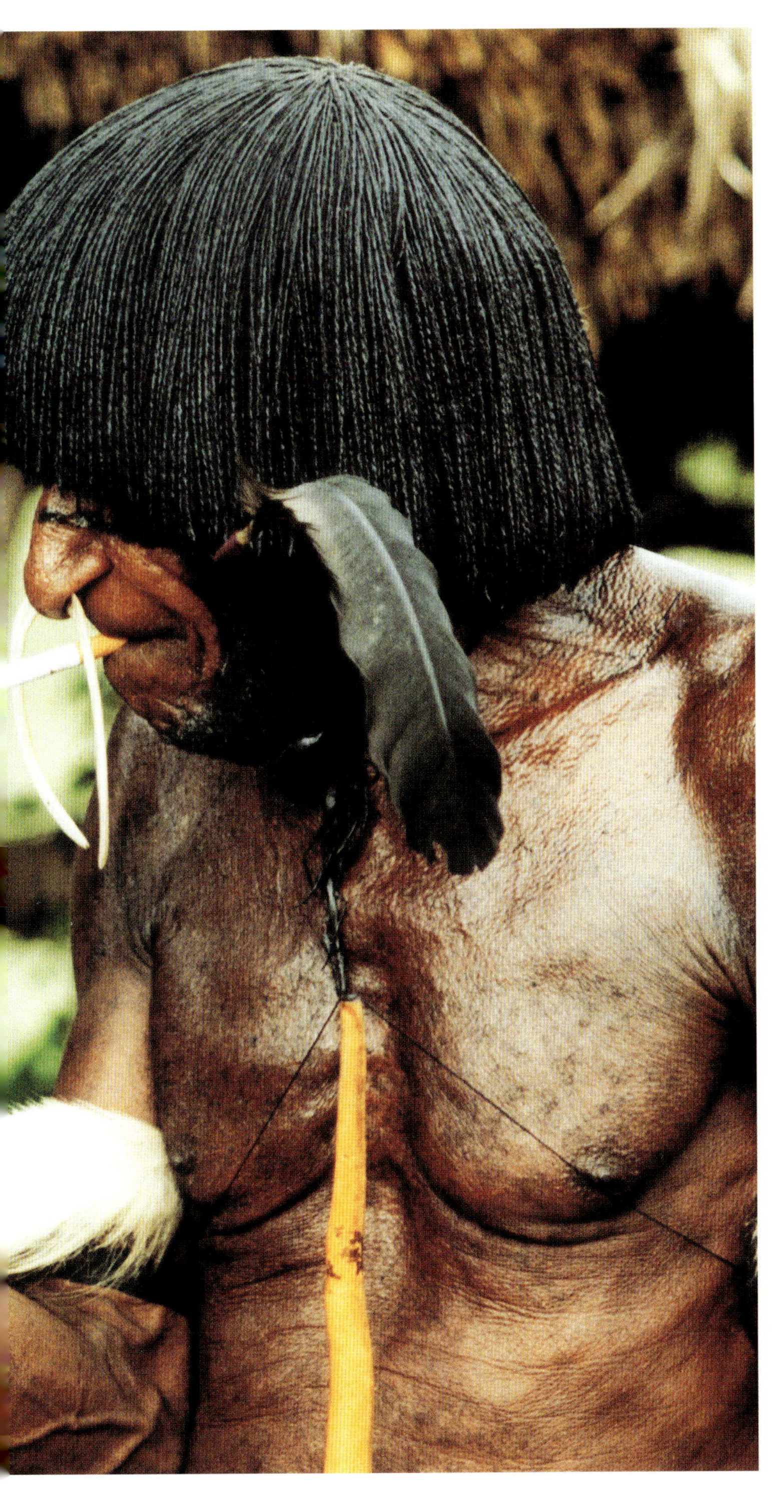

Many people will walk in and out of your life, but only true friends will leave **footprints** in your heart.

[ELEANOR ROOSEVELT]

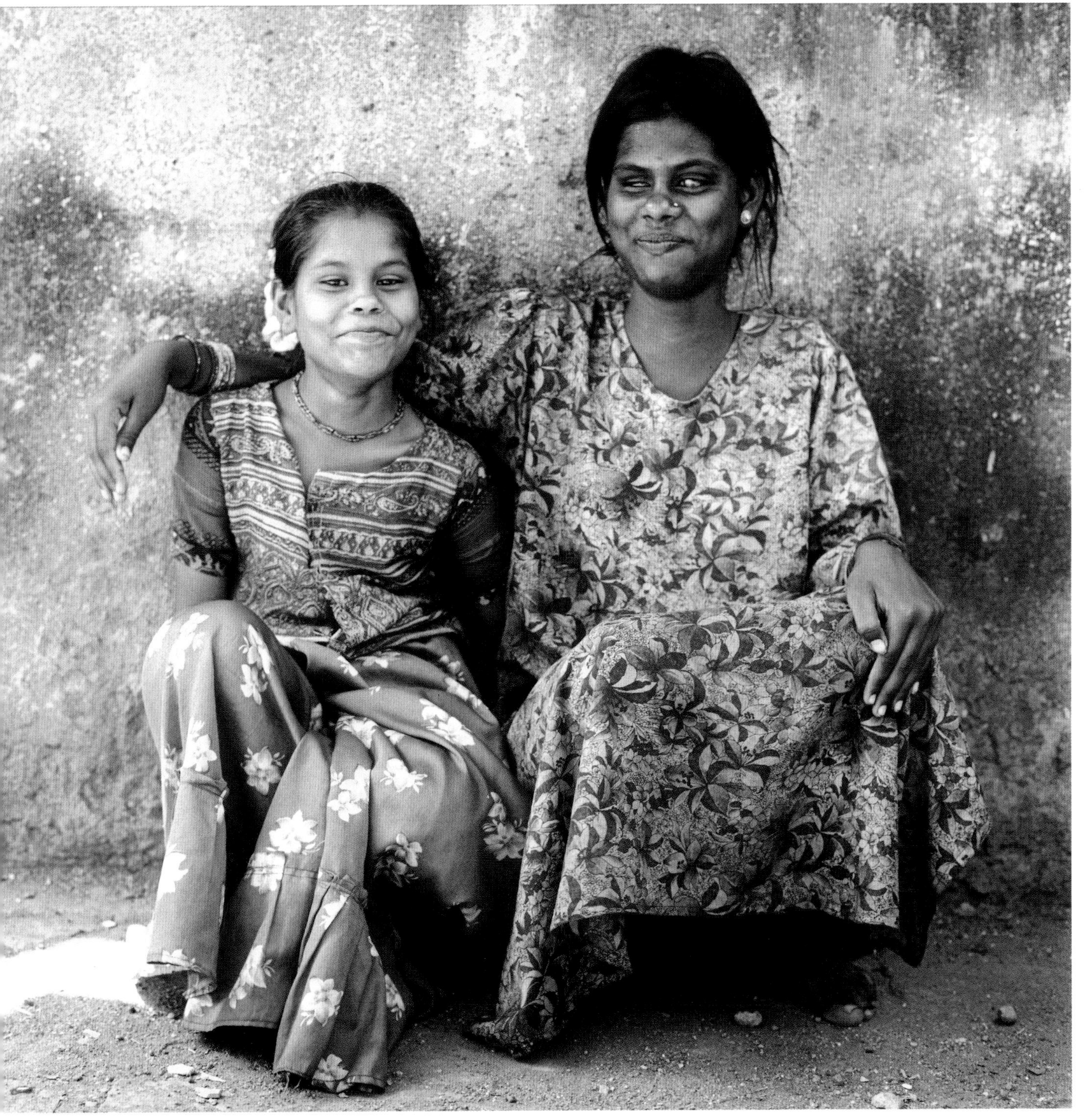

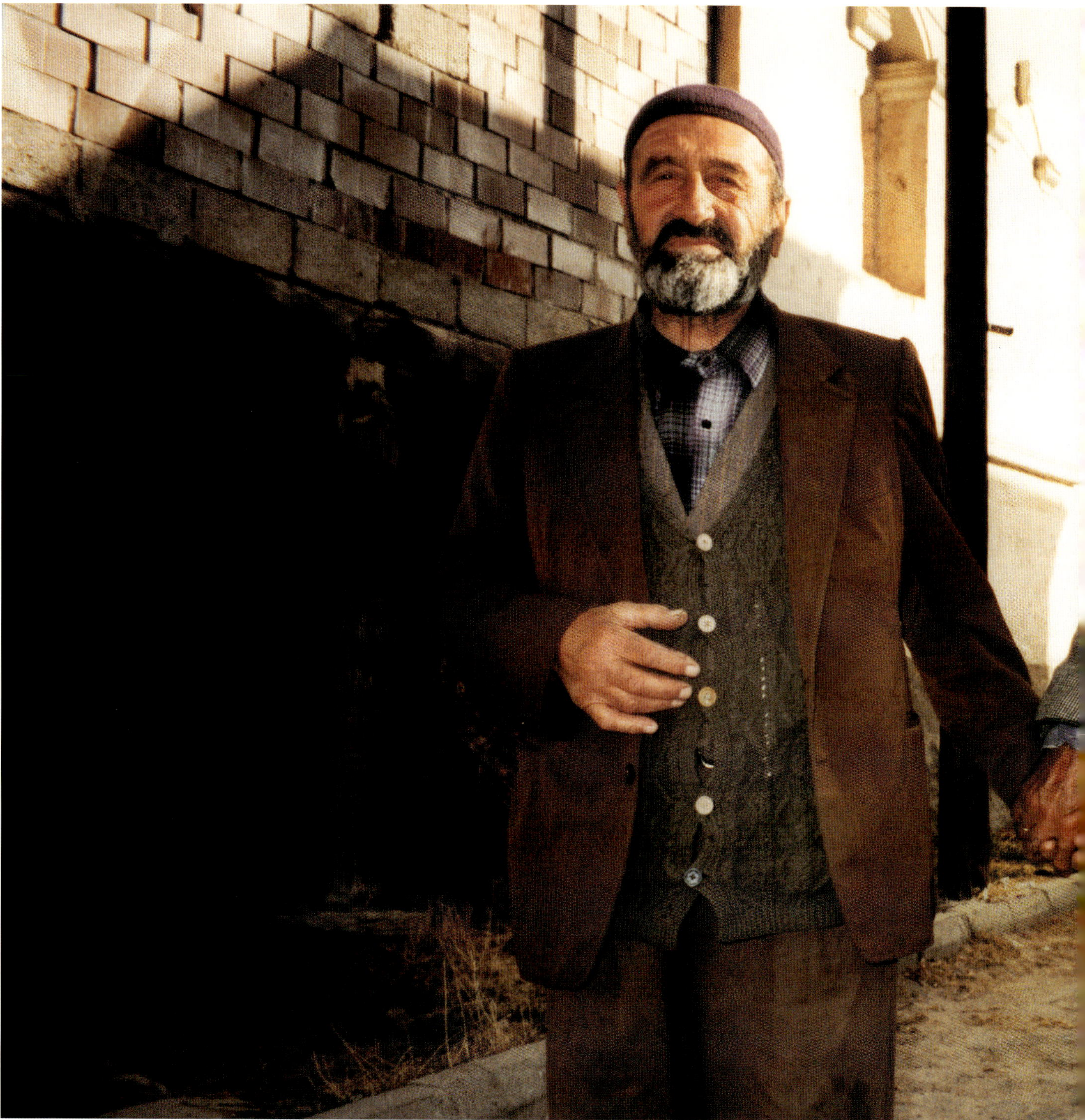

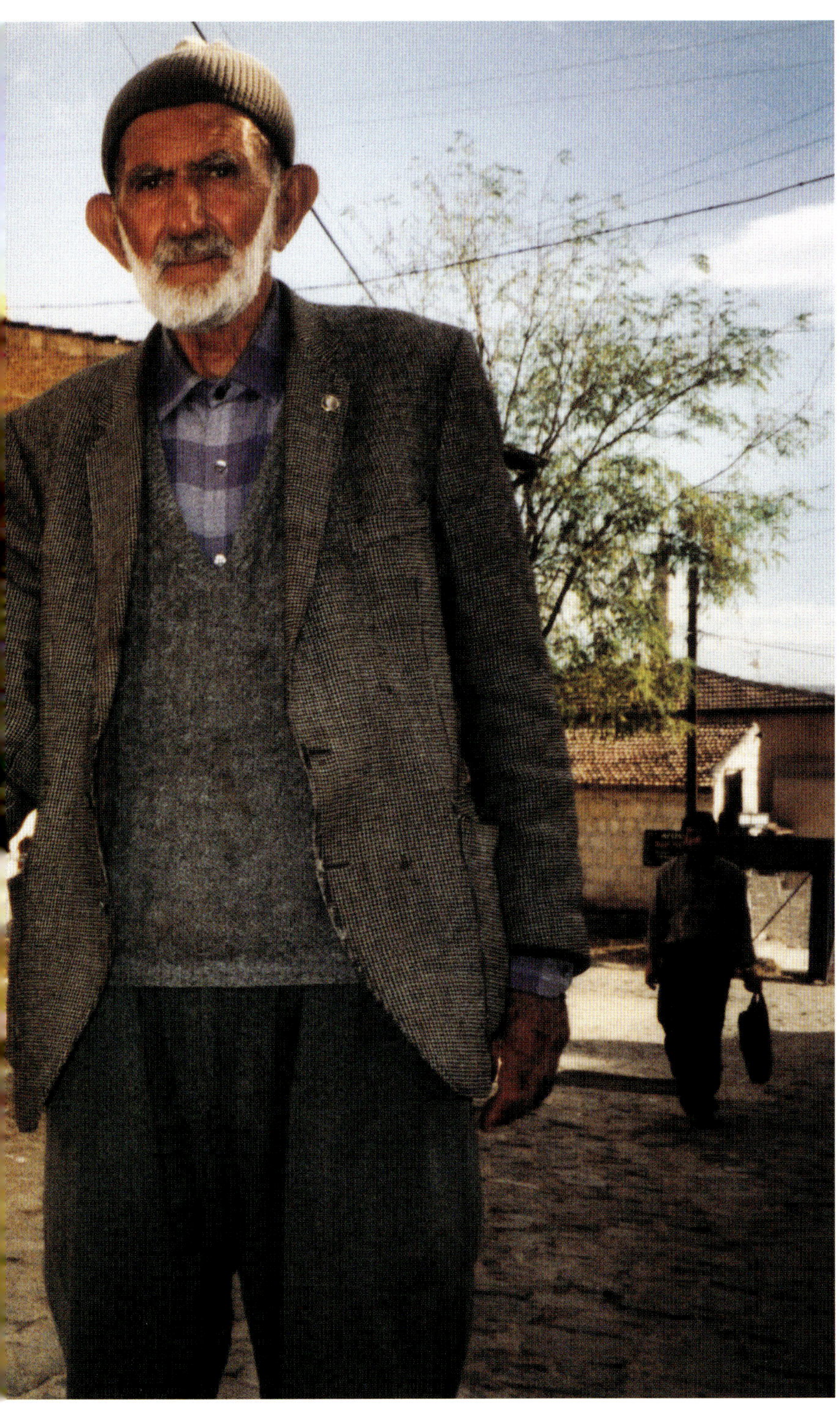

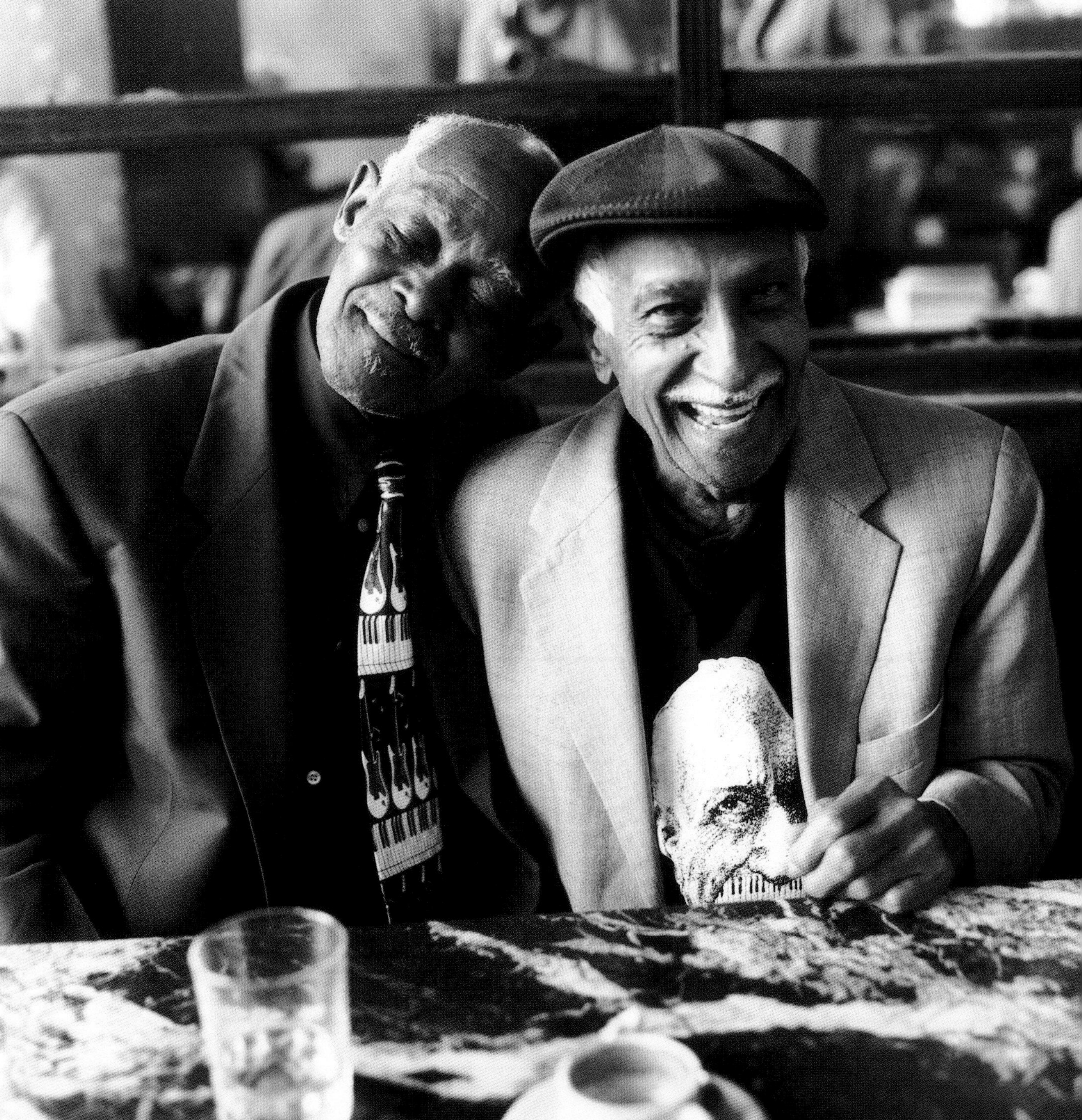

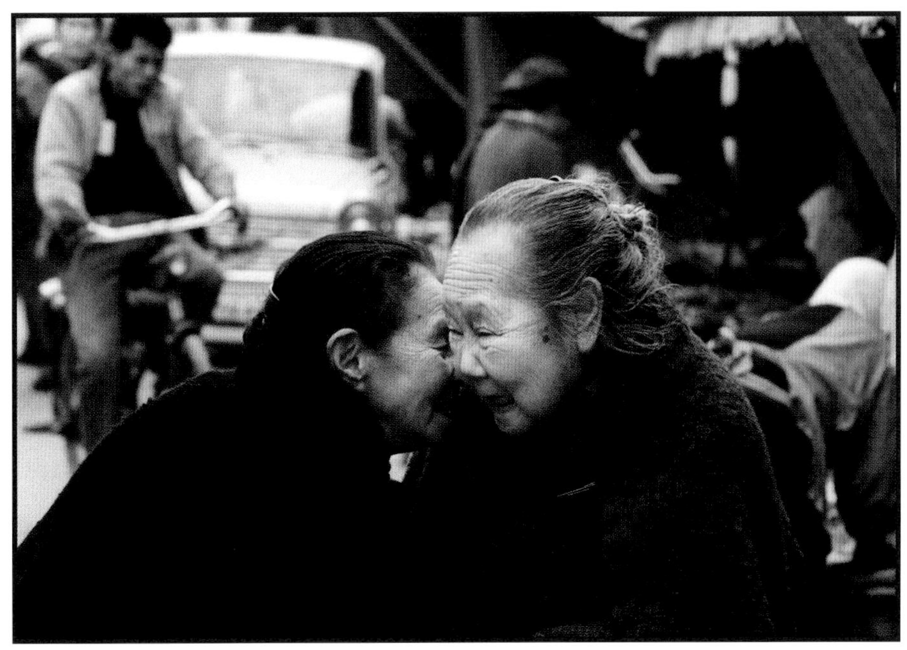

A single rose can be my garden... a single friend, my world.

[LEO BUSCAGLIA]

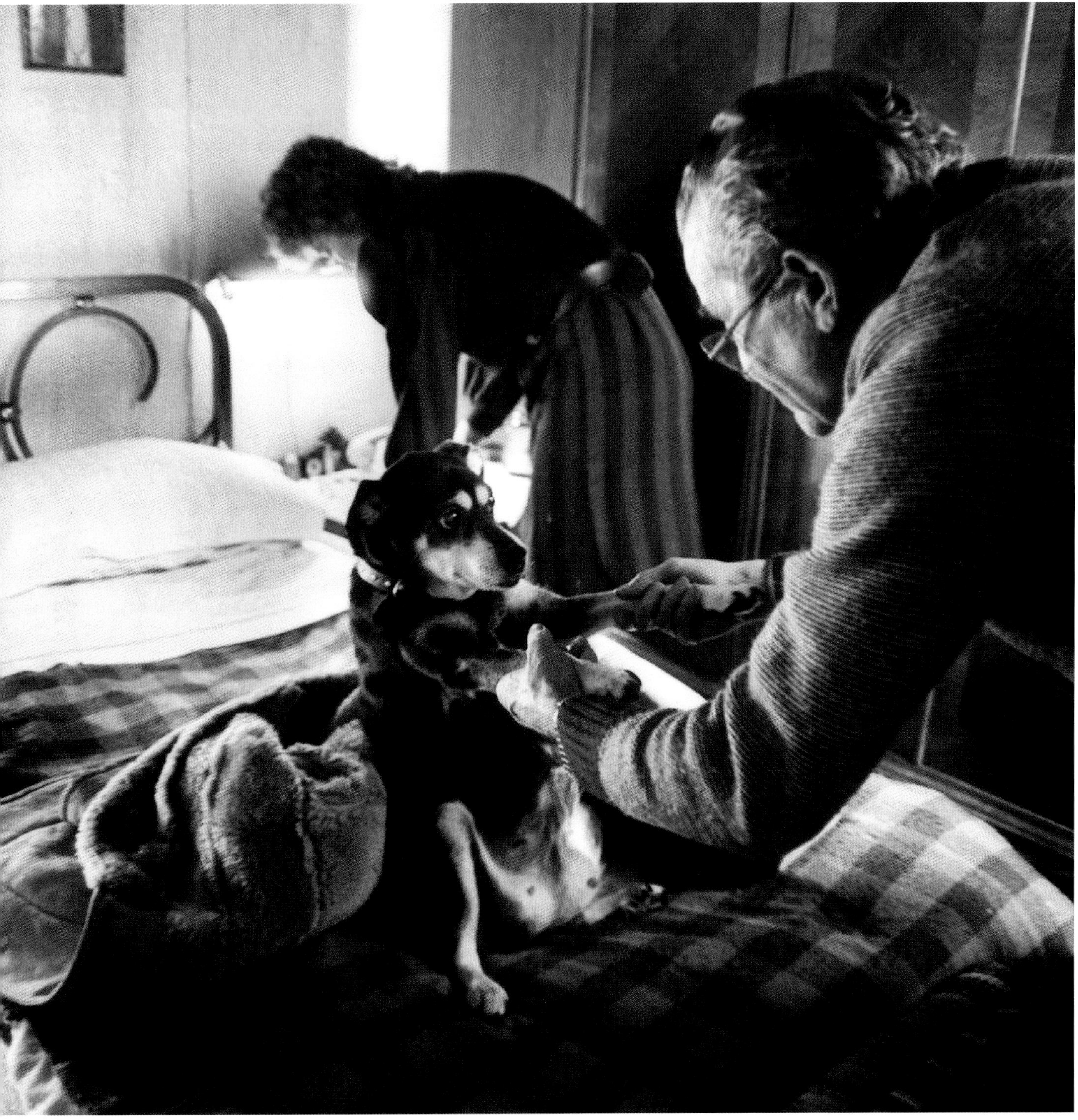

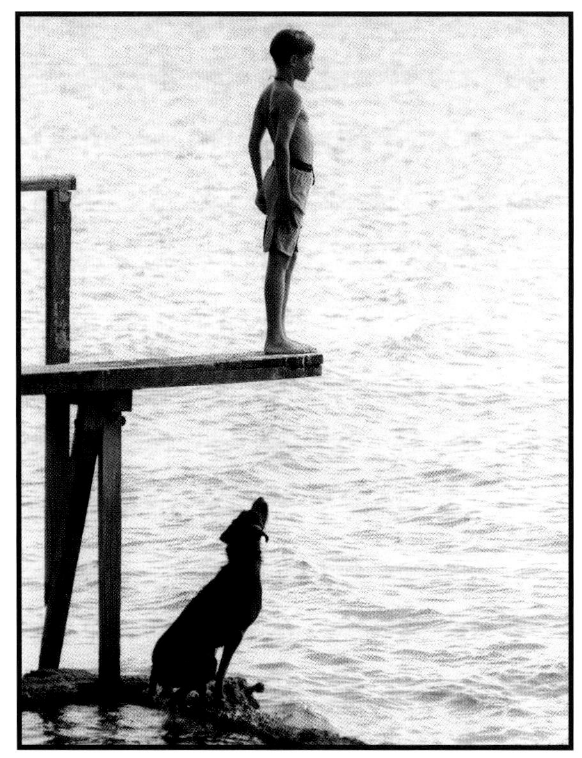

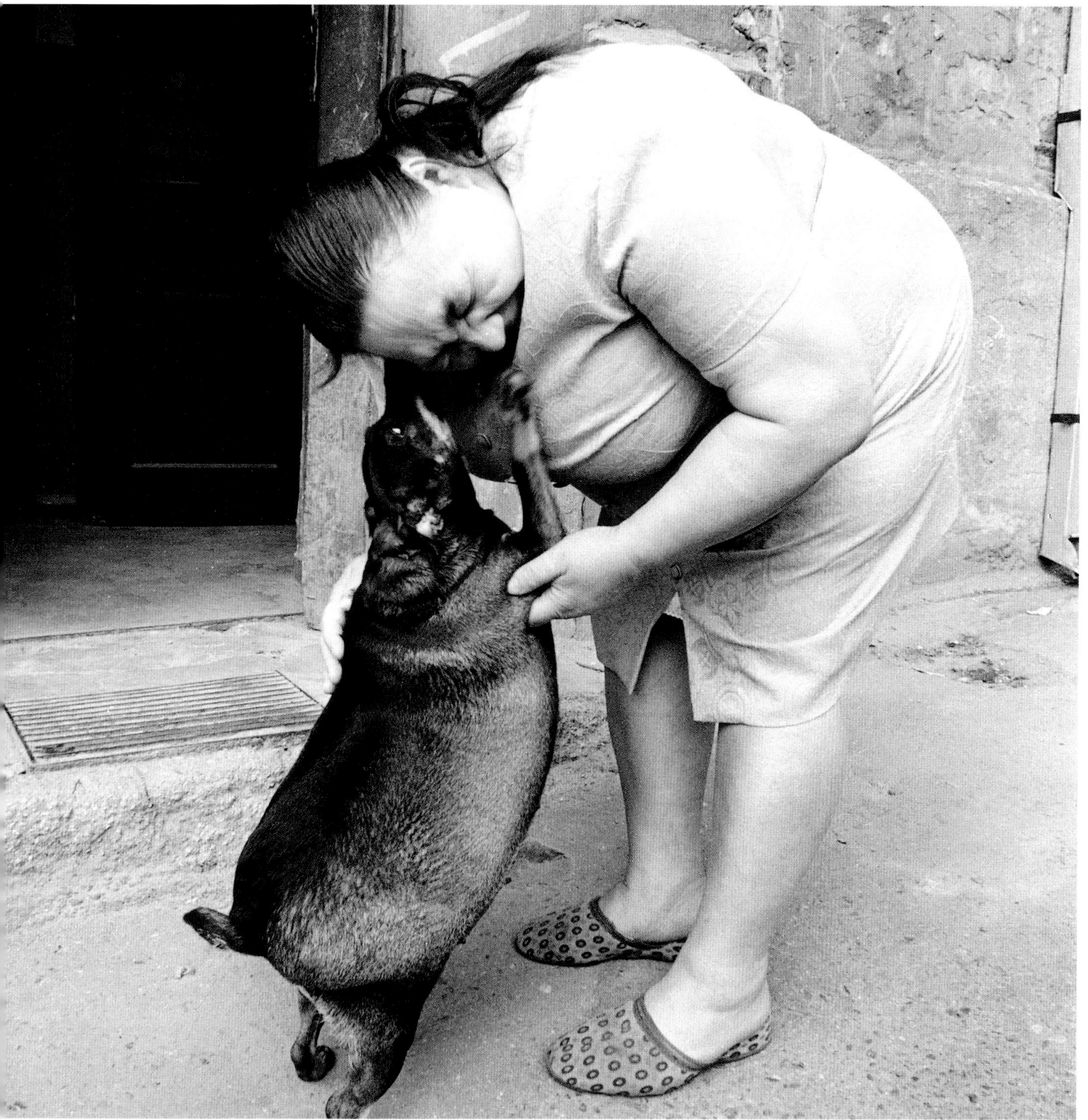

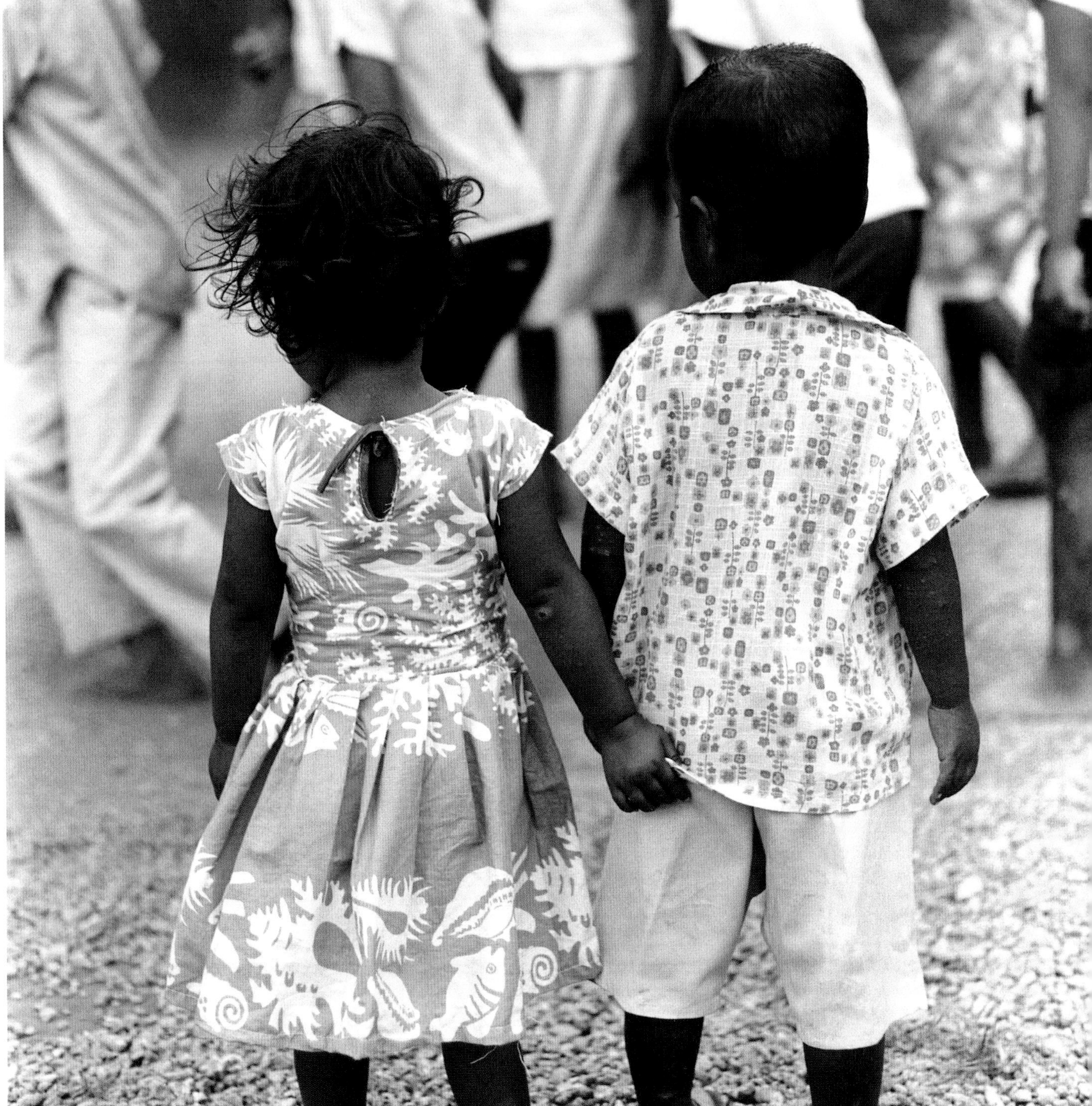

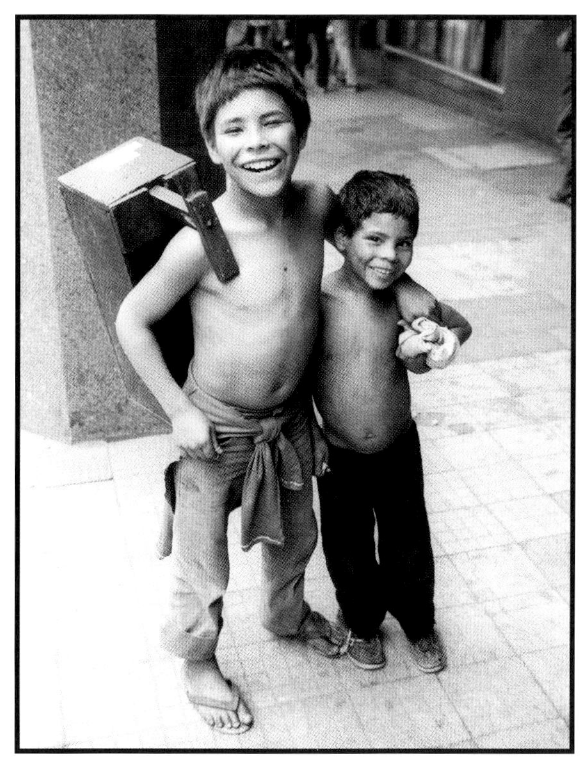

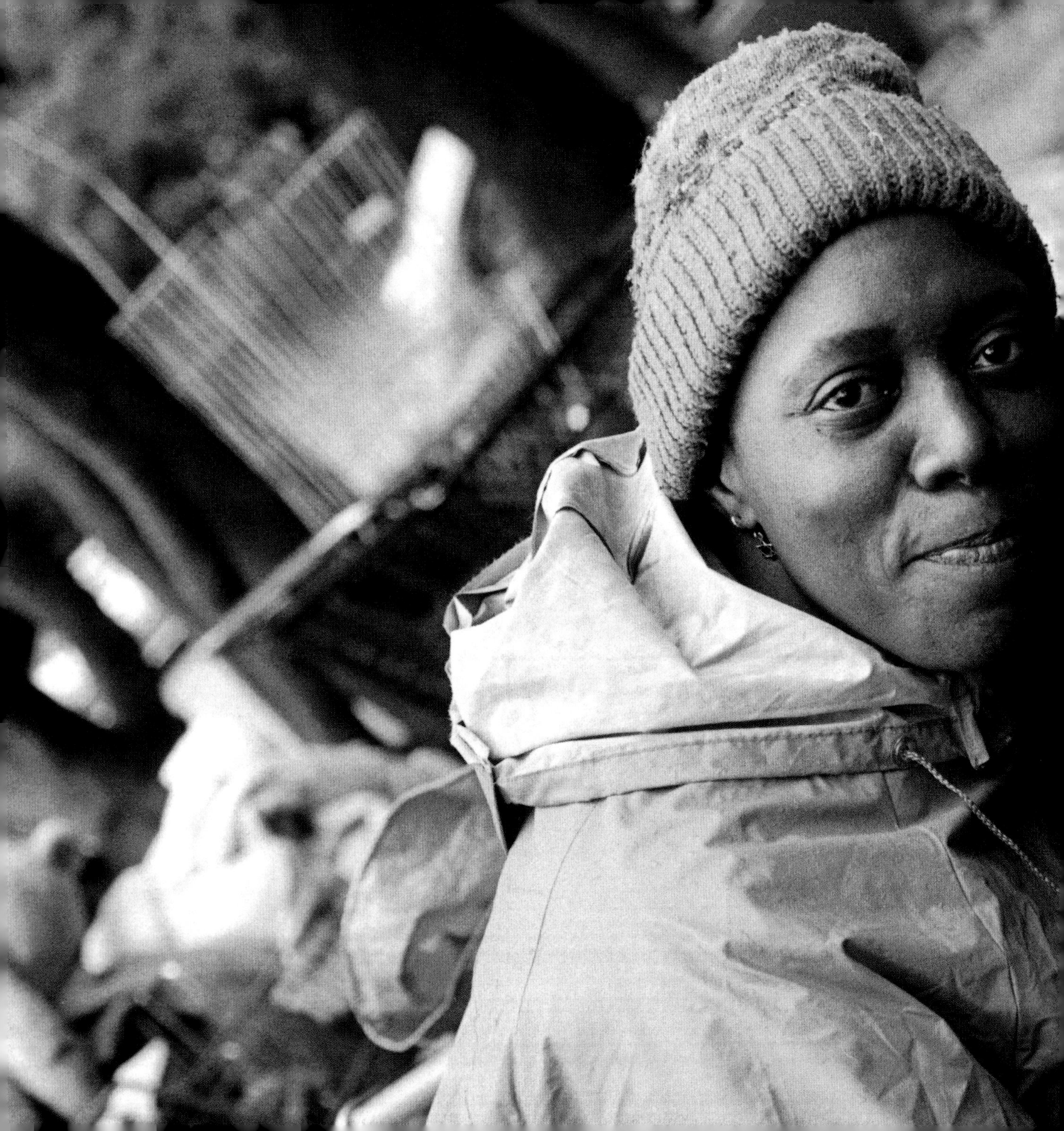

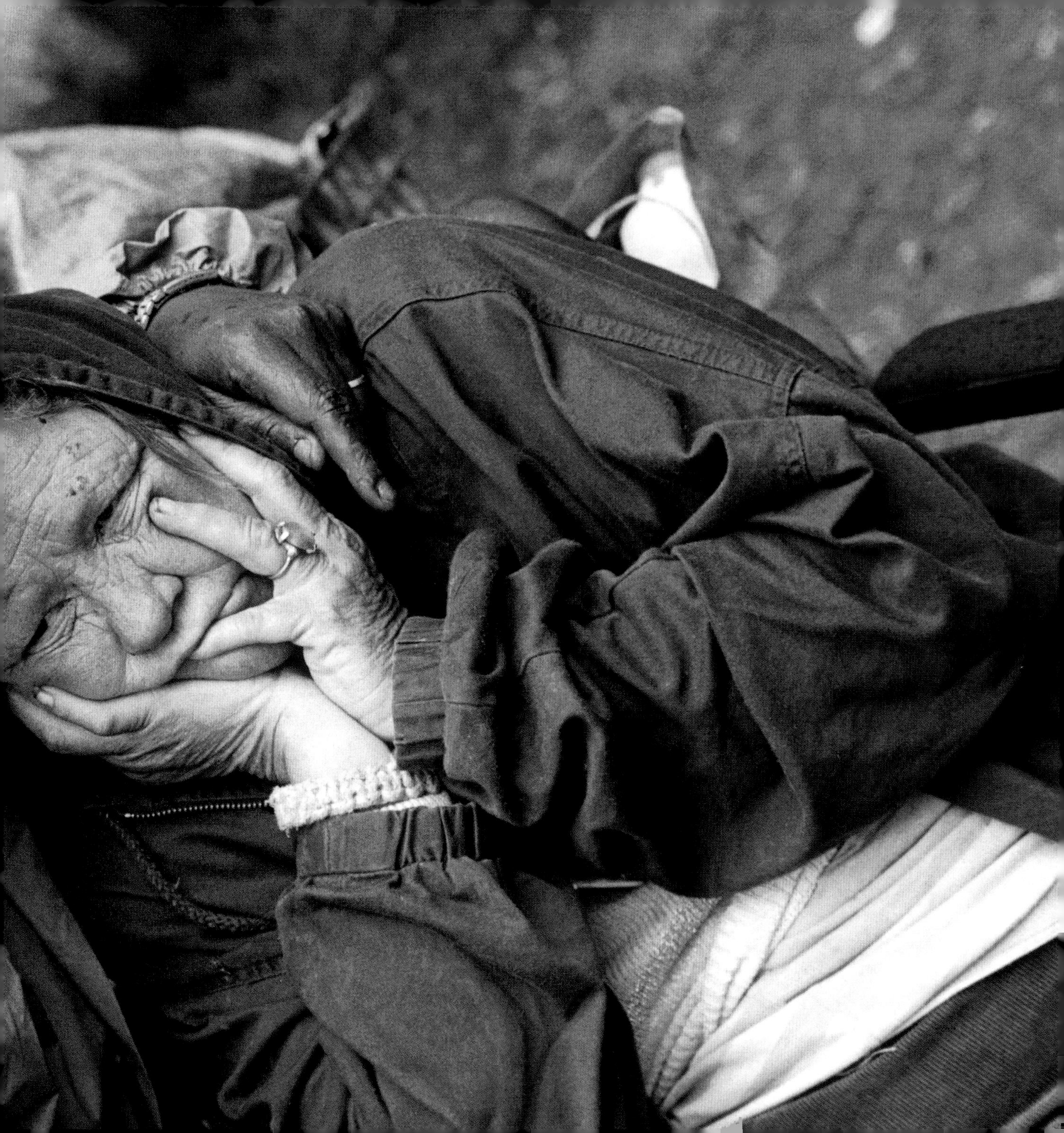

A friendship can grow on the most unlikely and barren ground.

[MAEVE BINCHY]

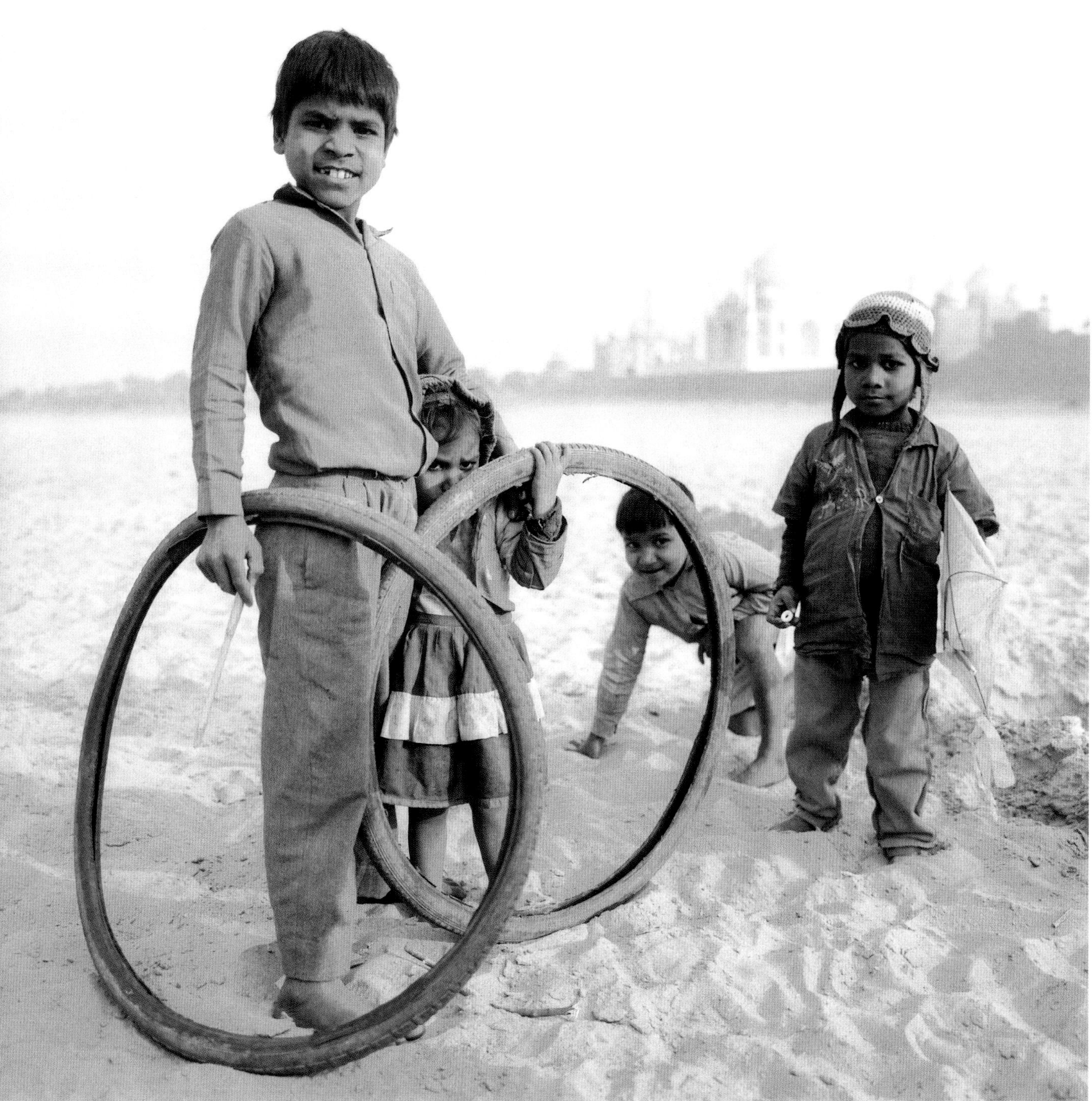

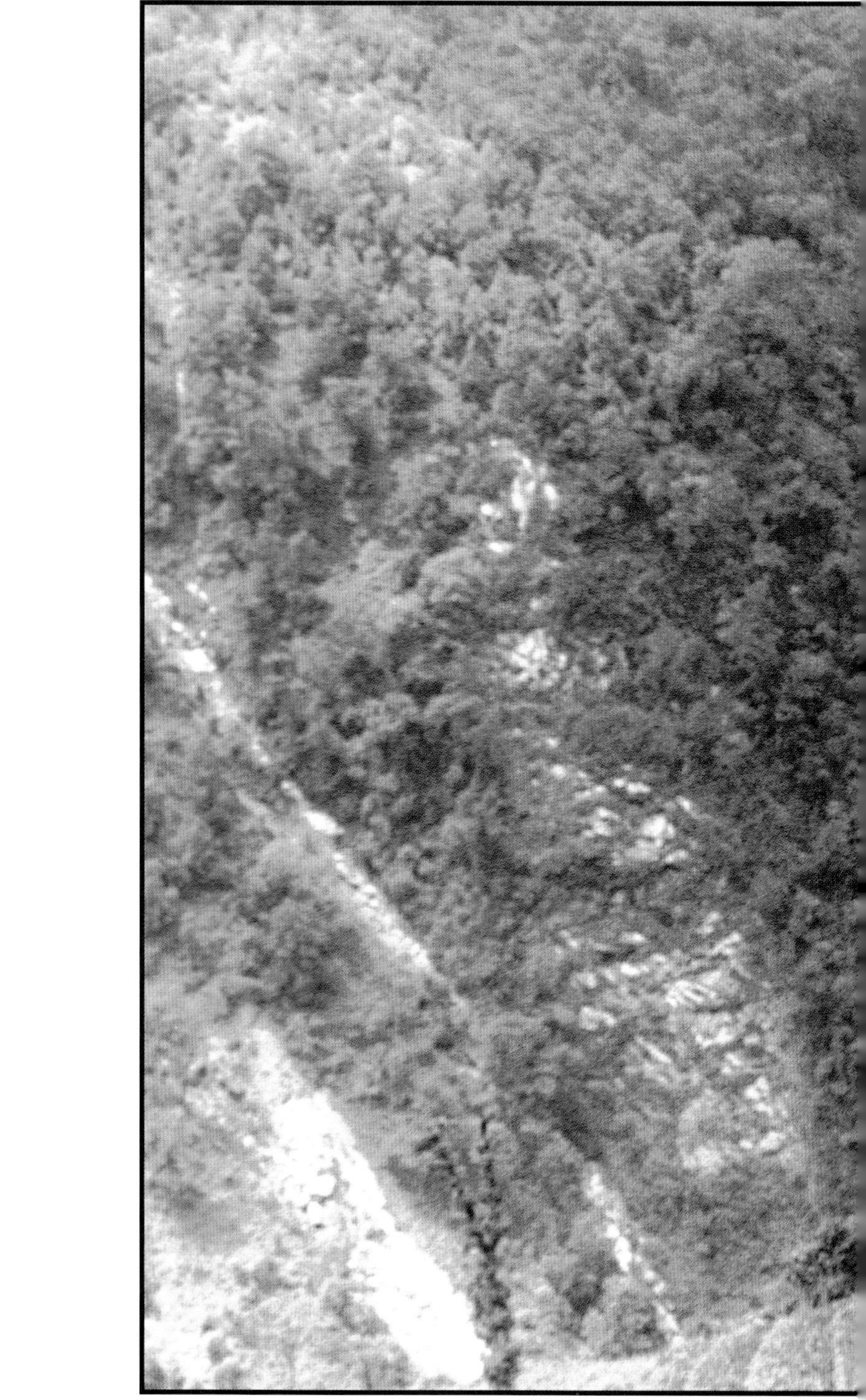

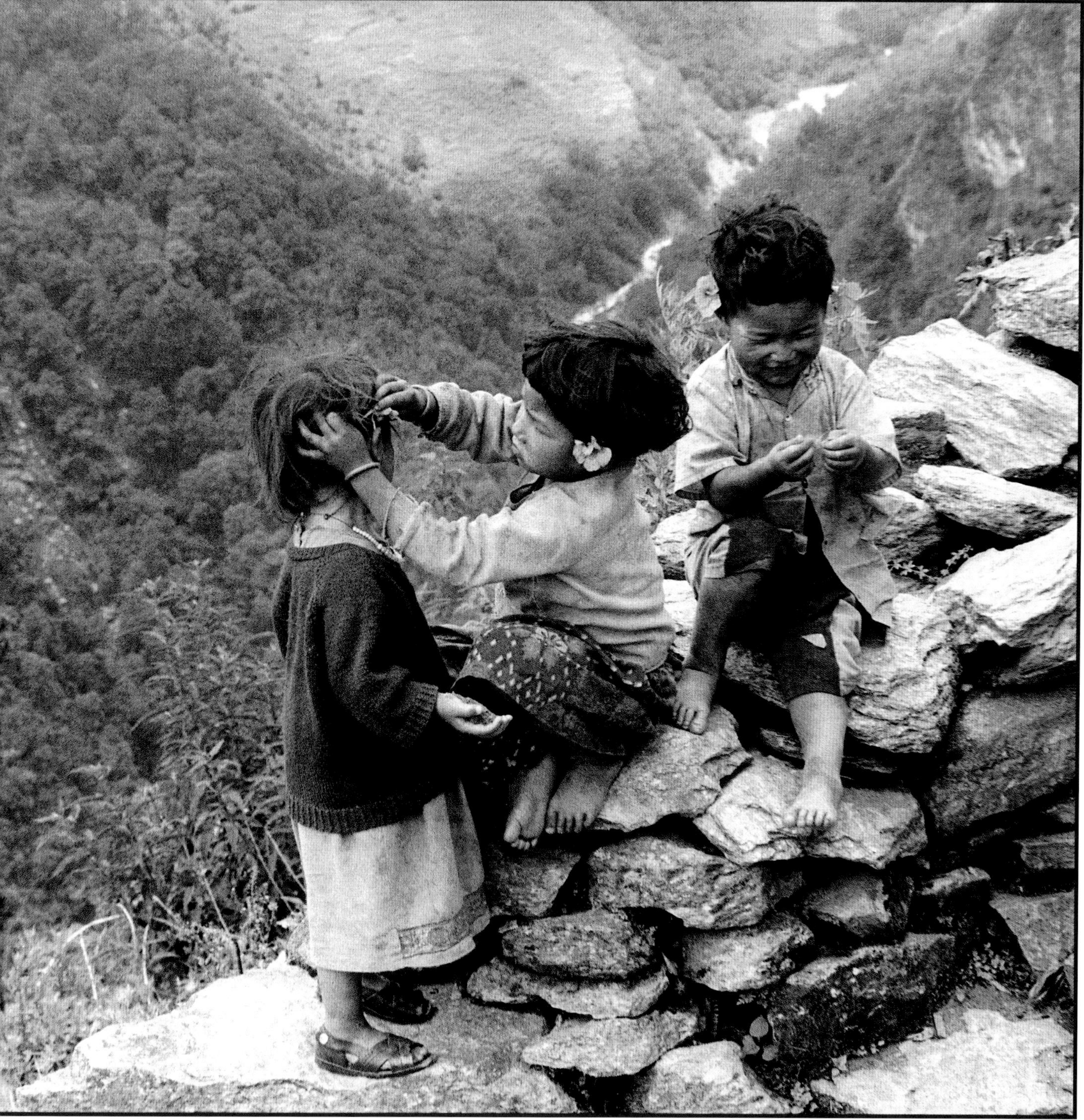

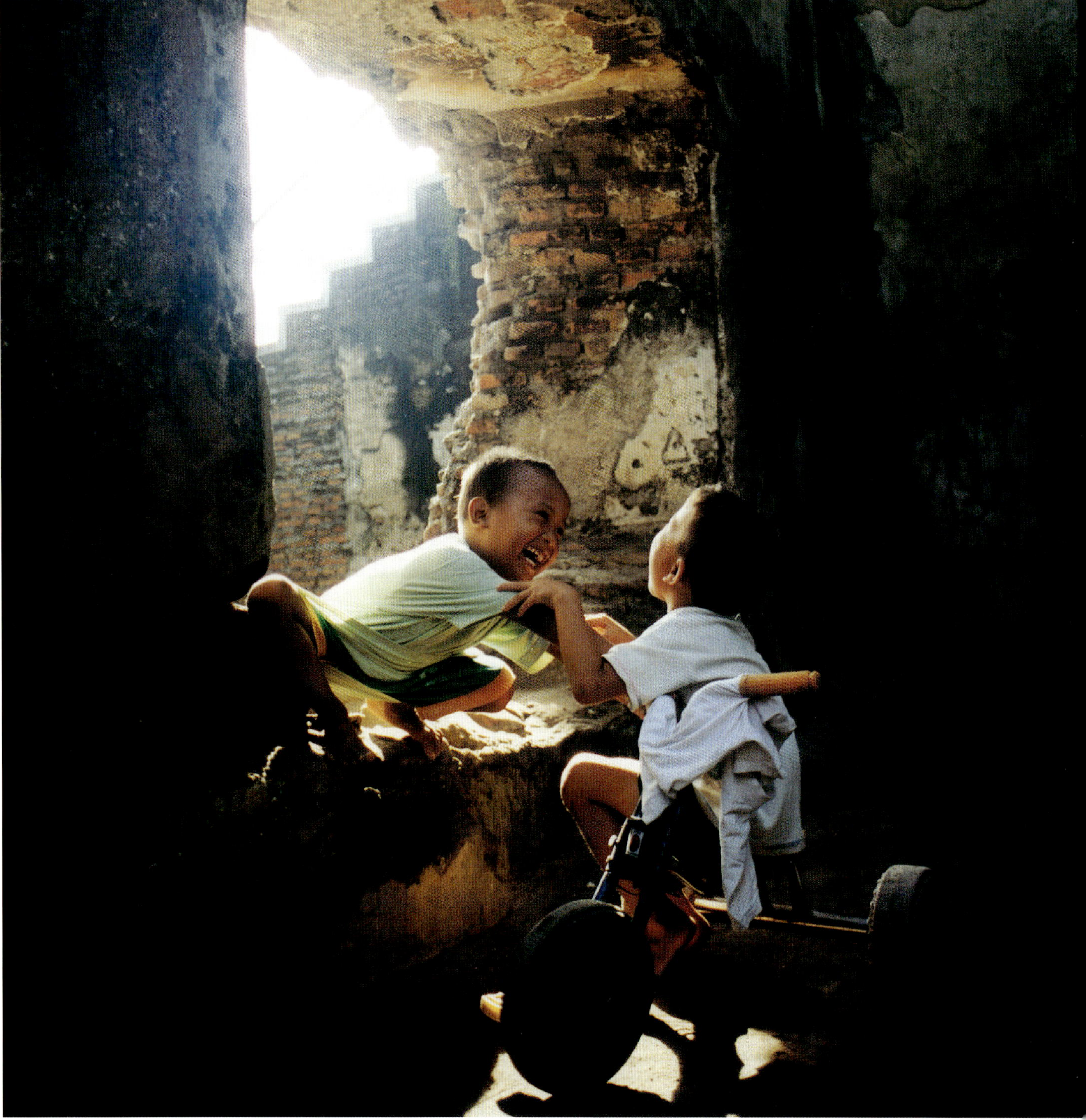

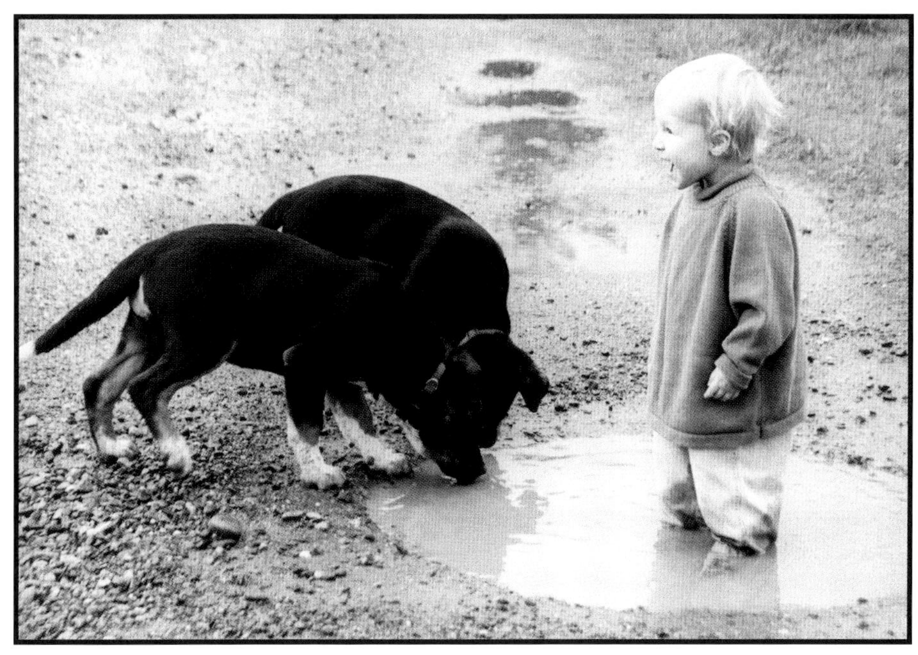

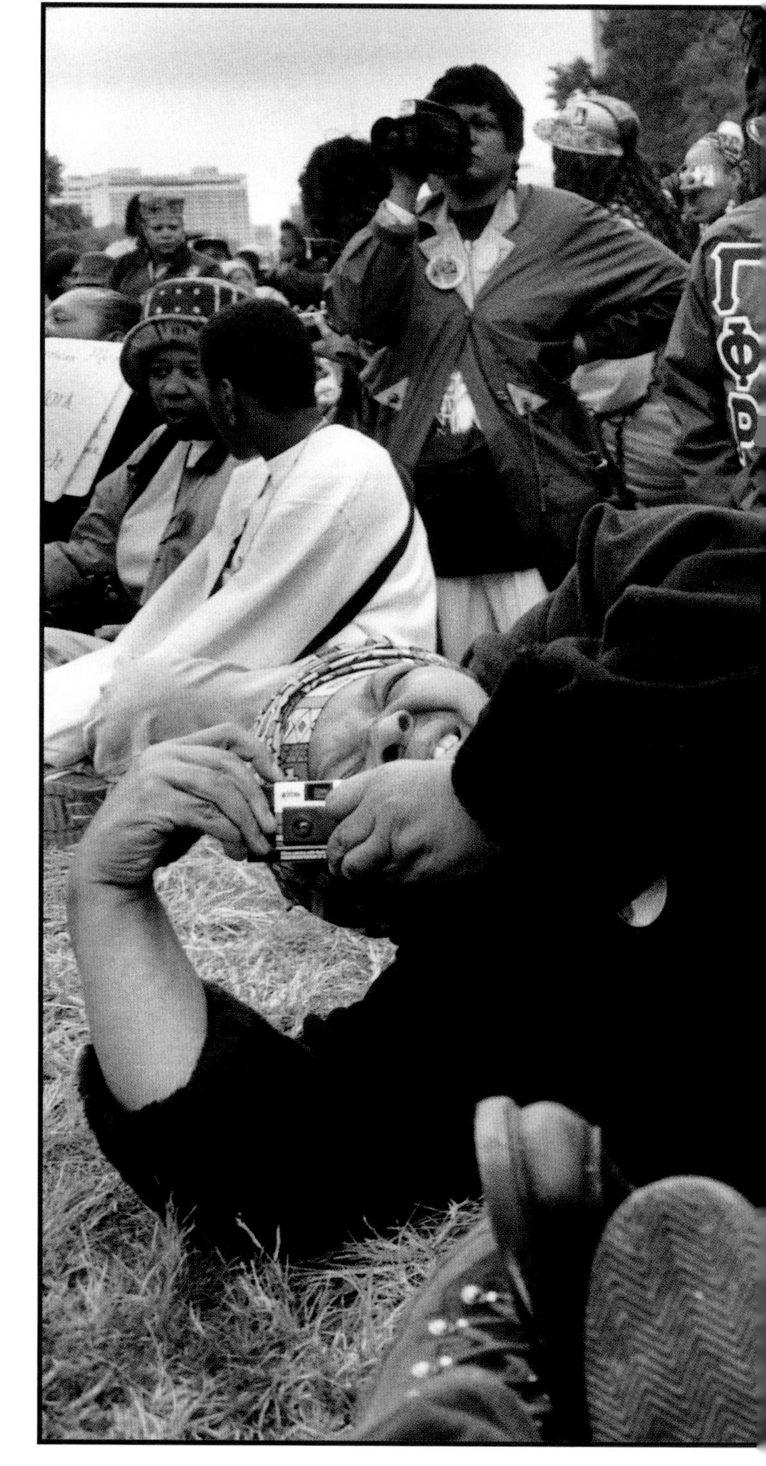

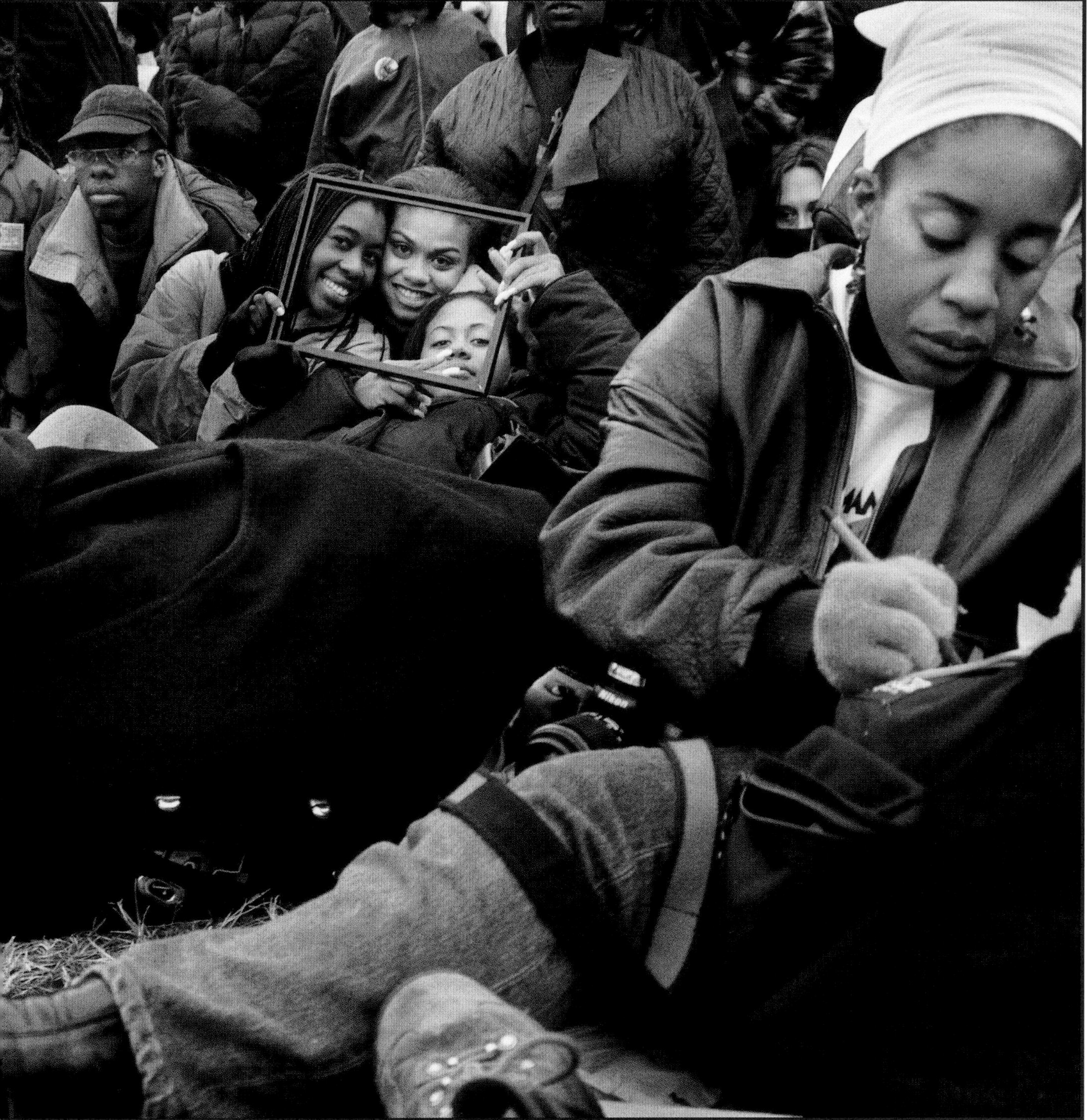

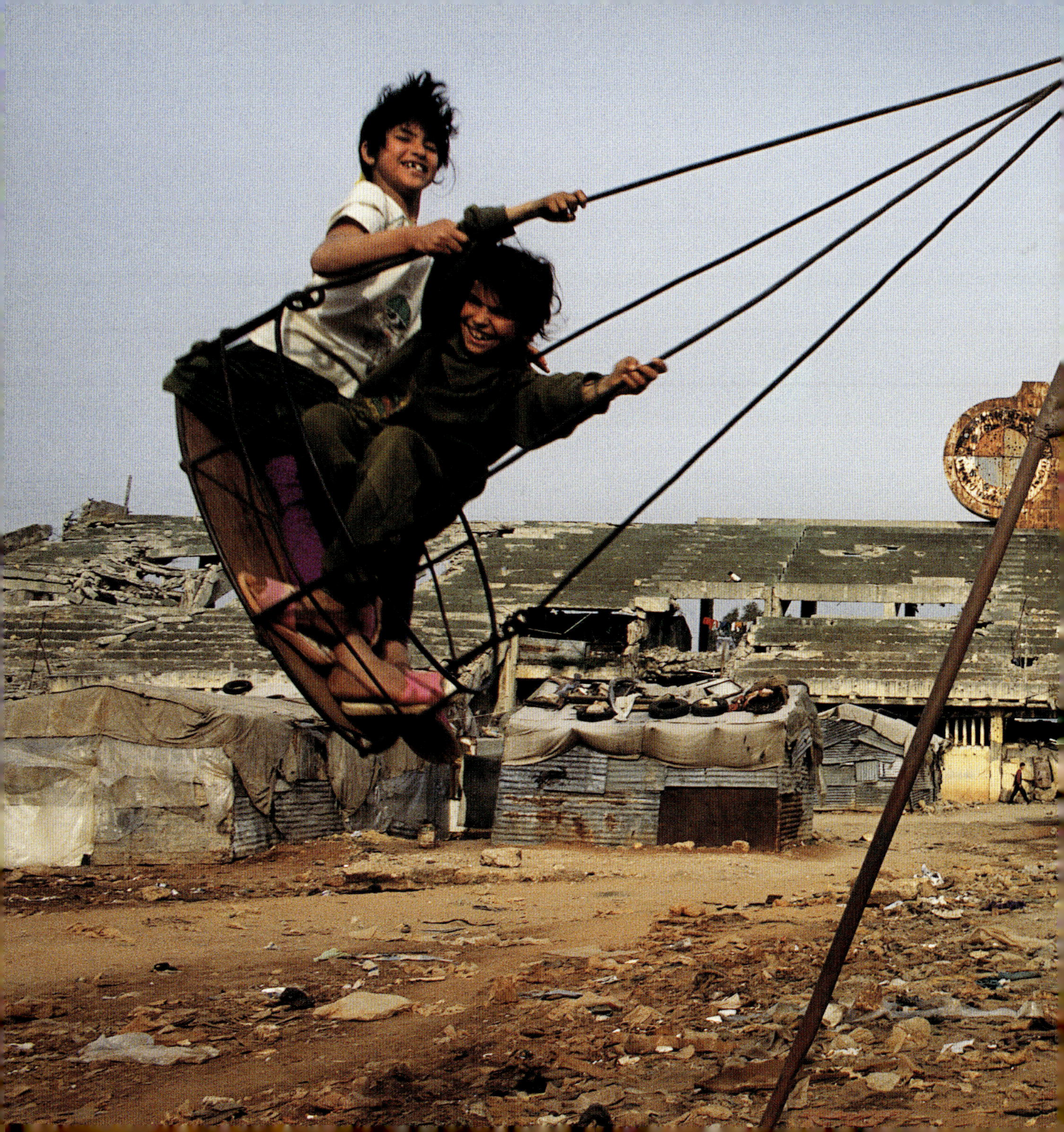

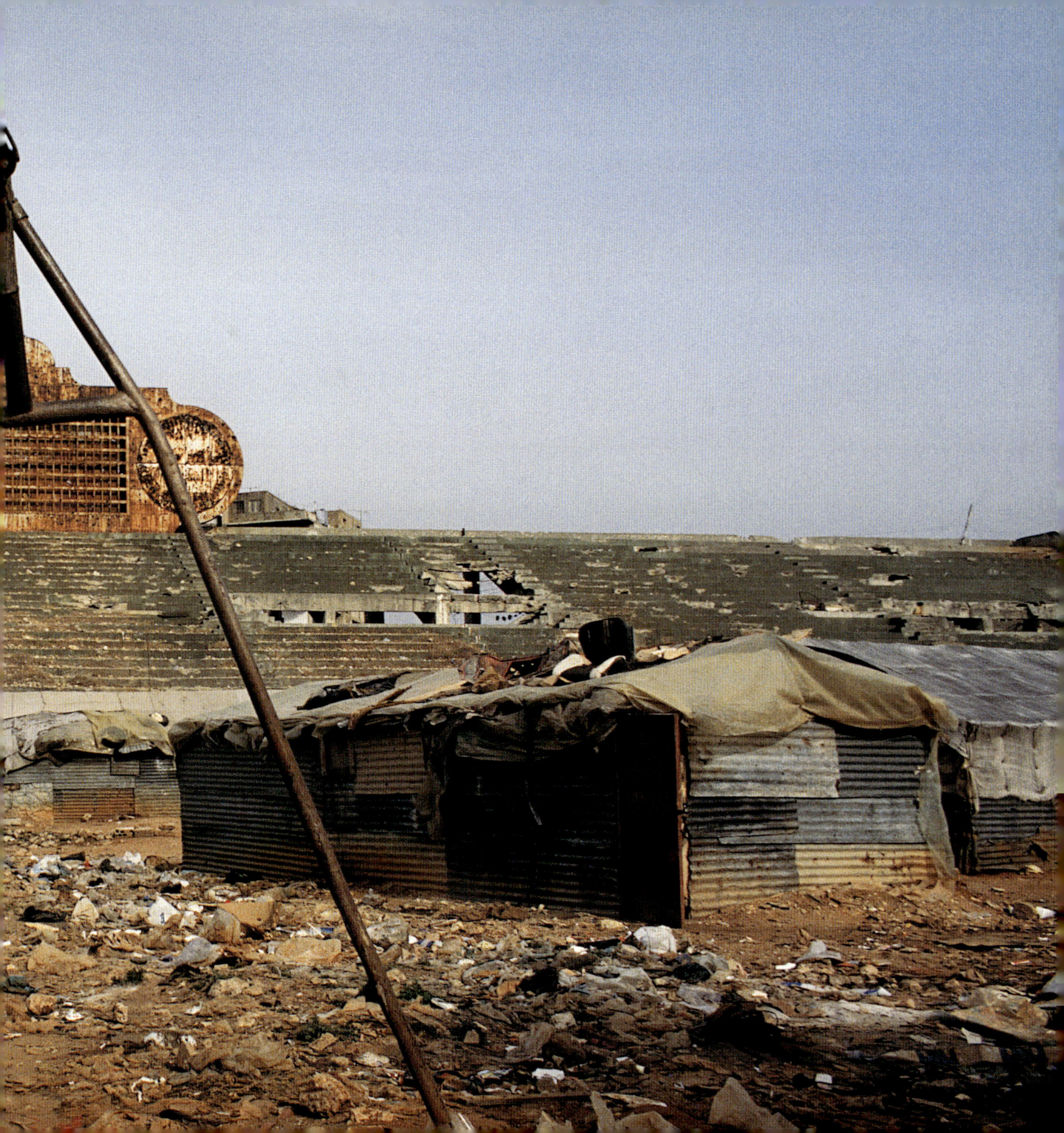

Good times made better and bad times forgotten due to
the **healing** magic of friendship.

[MAEVE BINCHY]

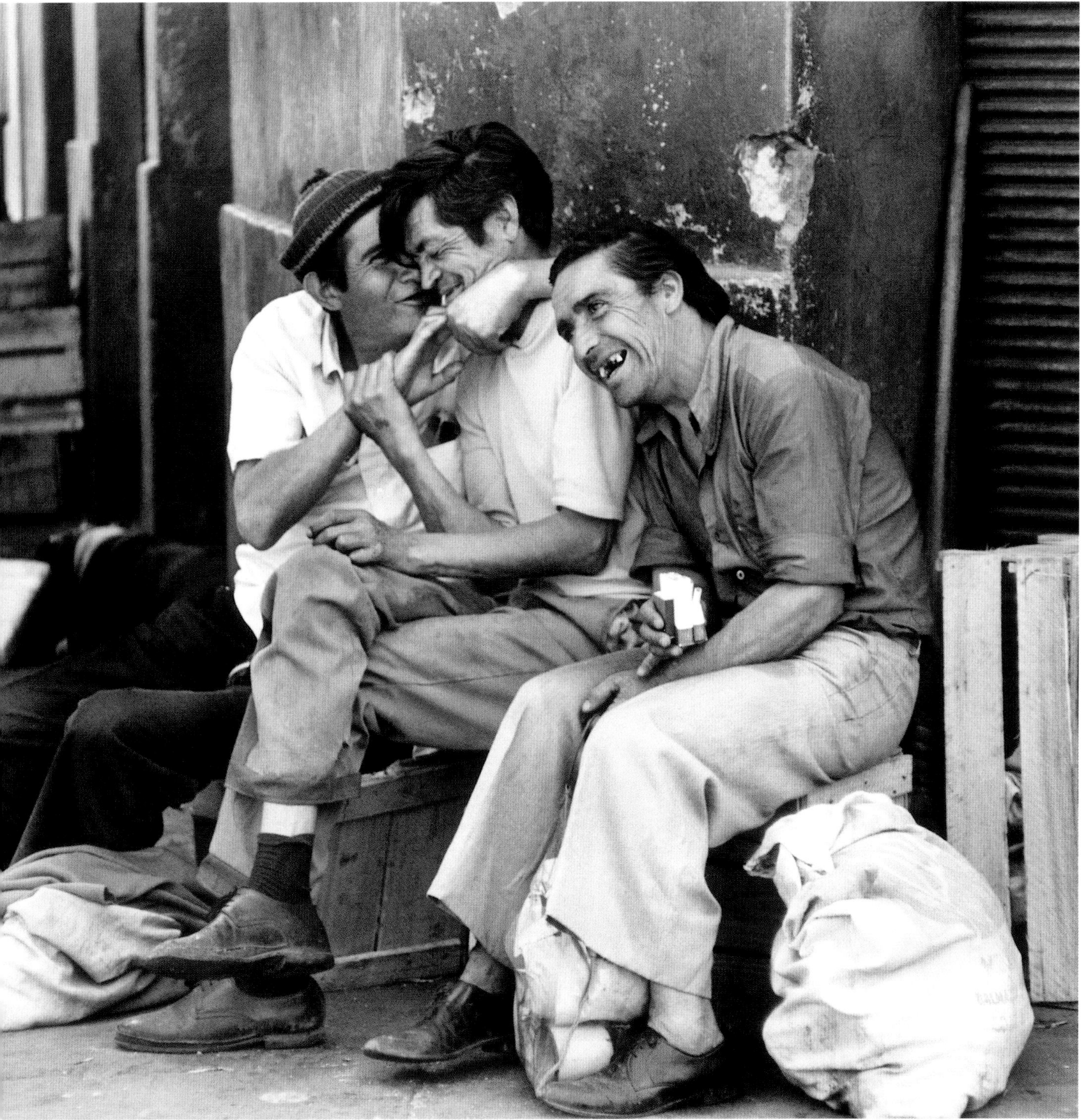

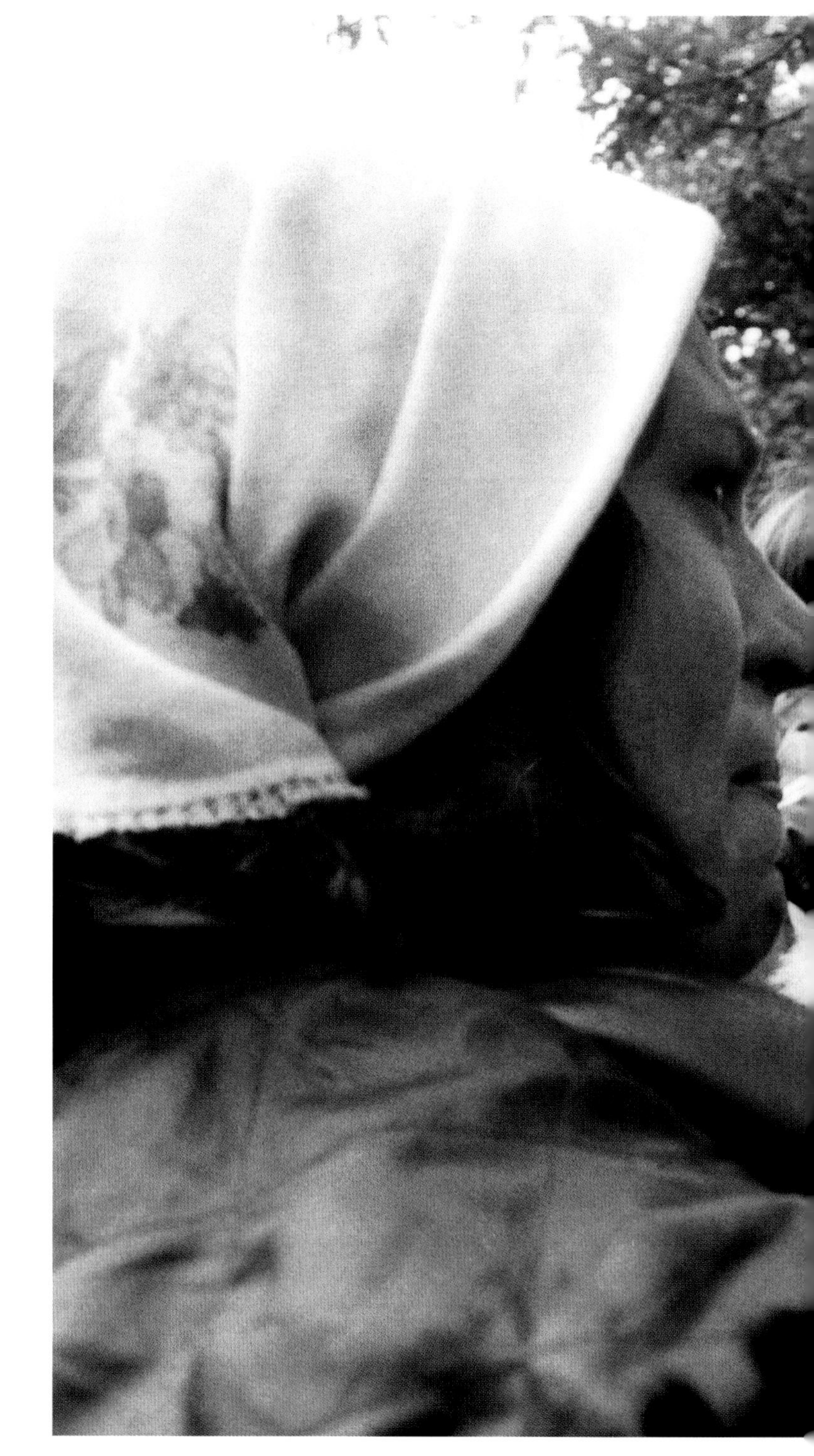

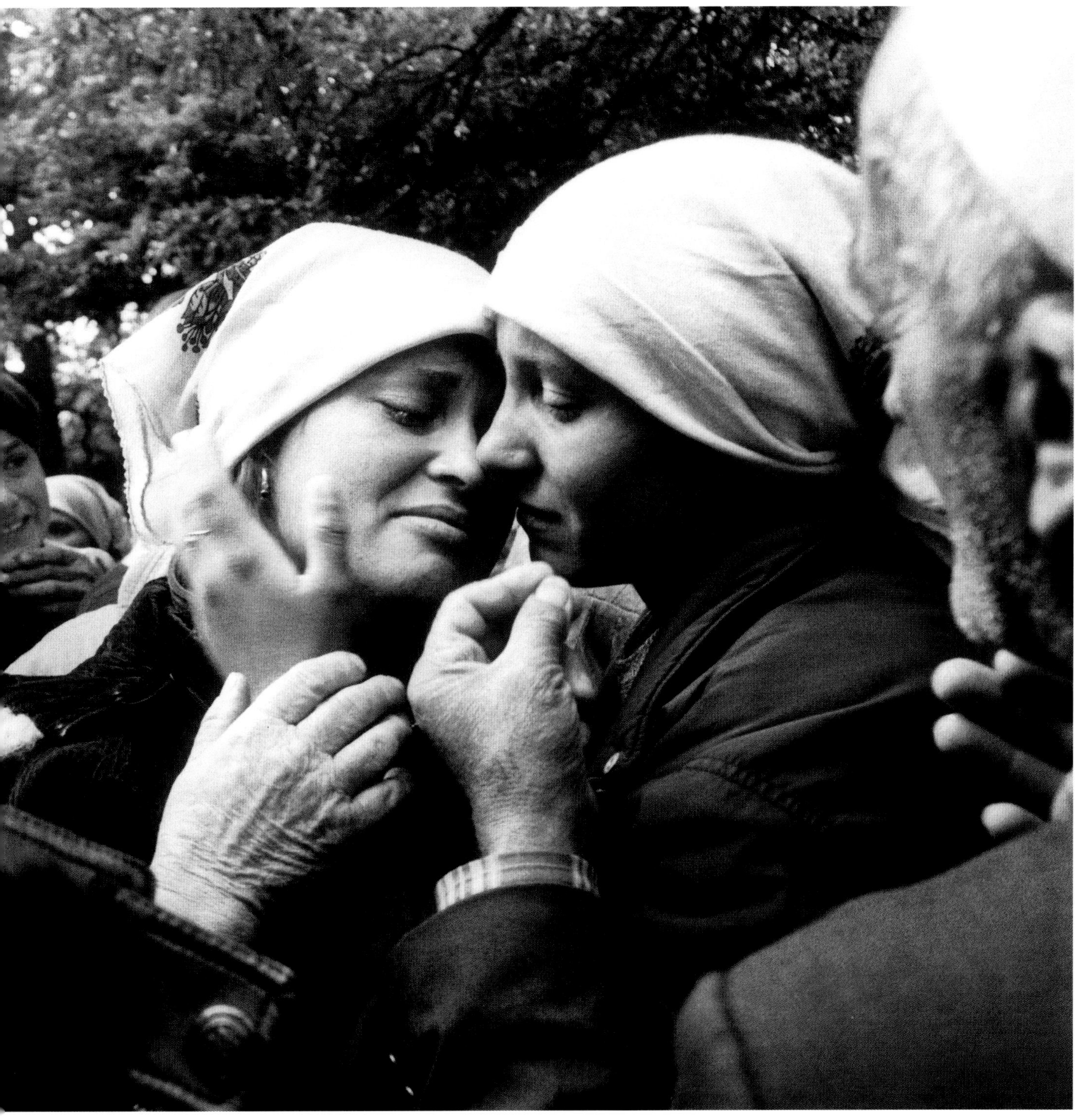

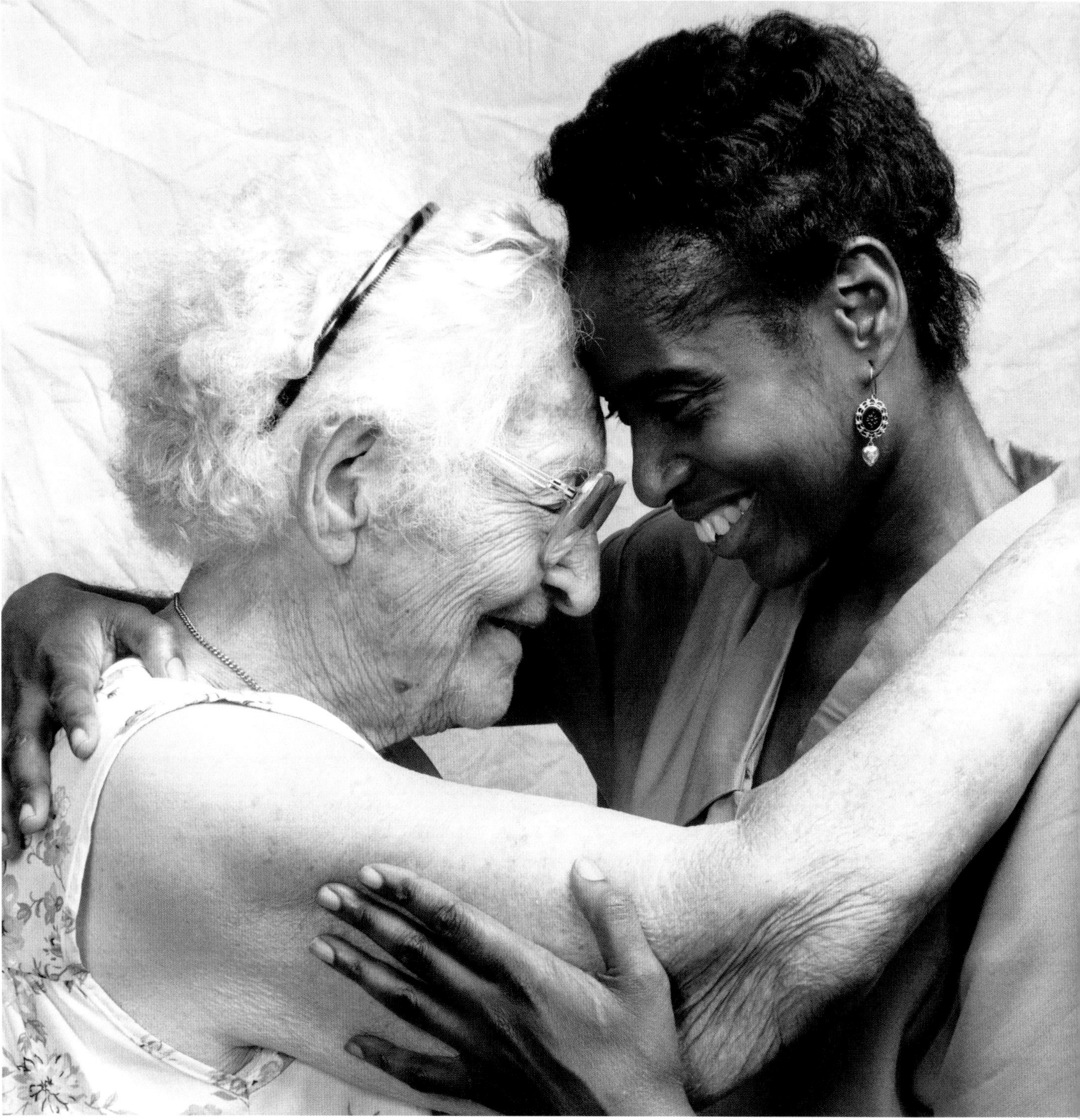

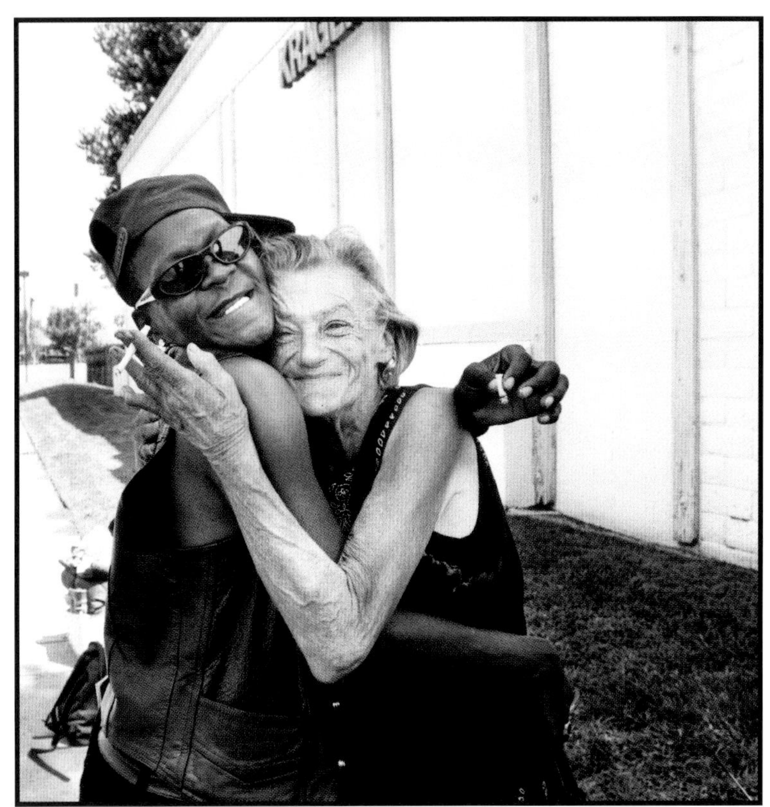

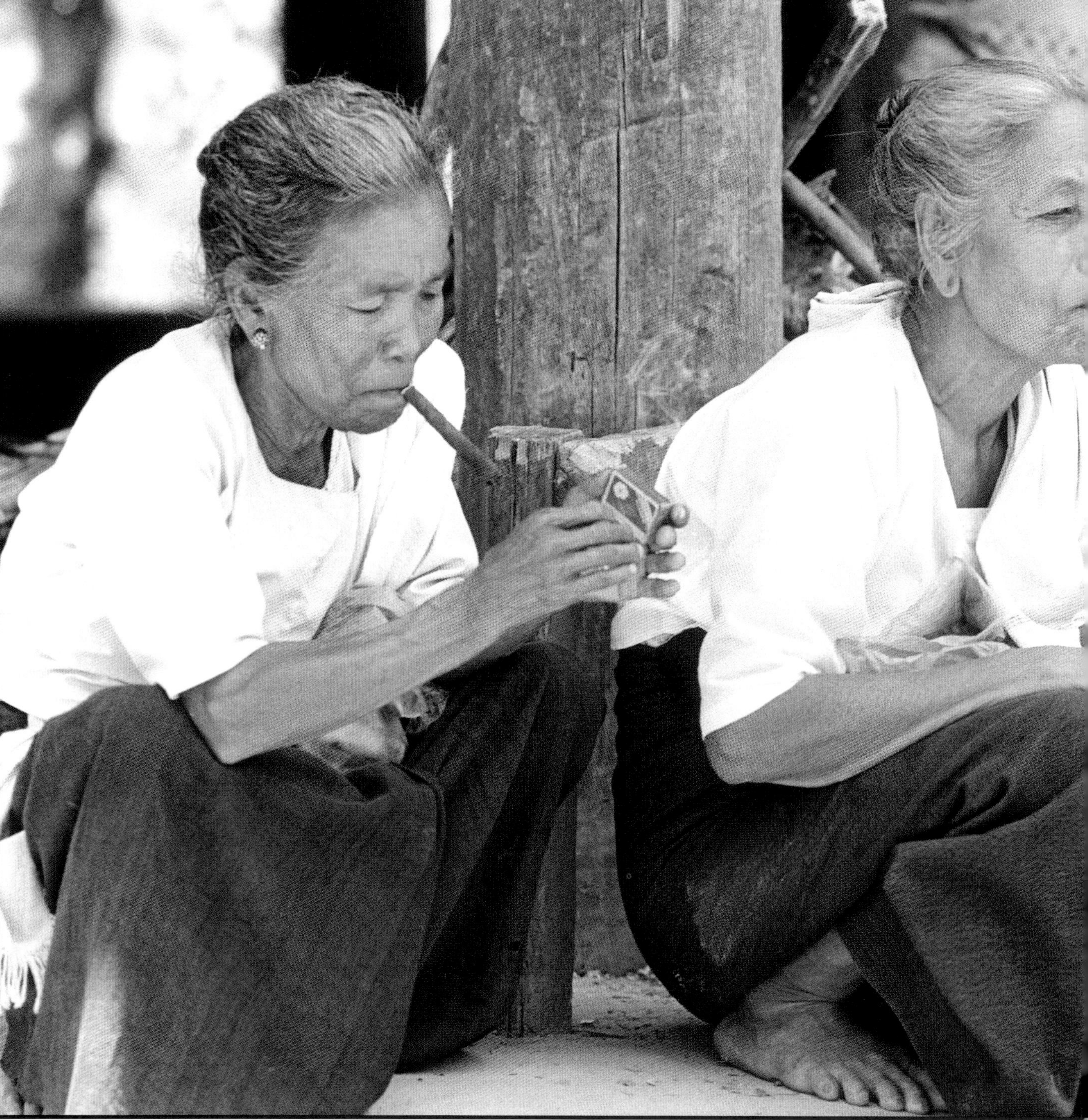

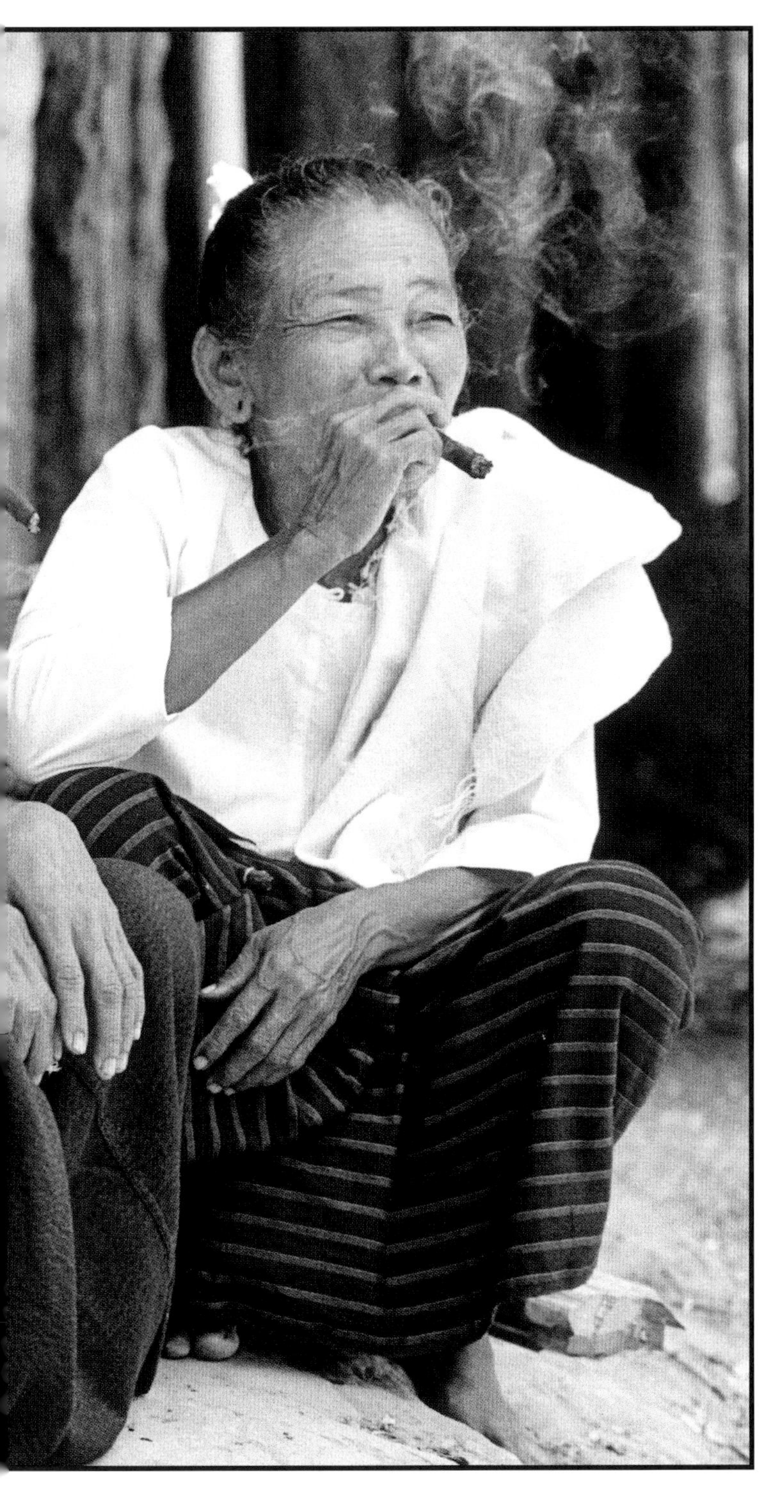

Without the human community one single human being cannot survive.

[DALAI LAMA]

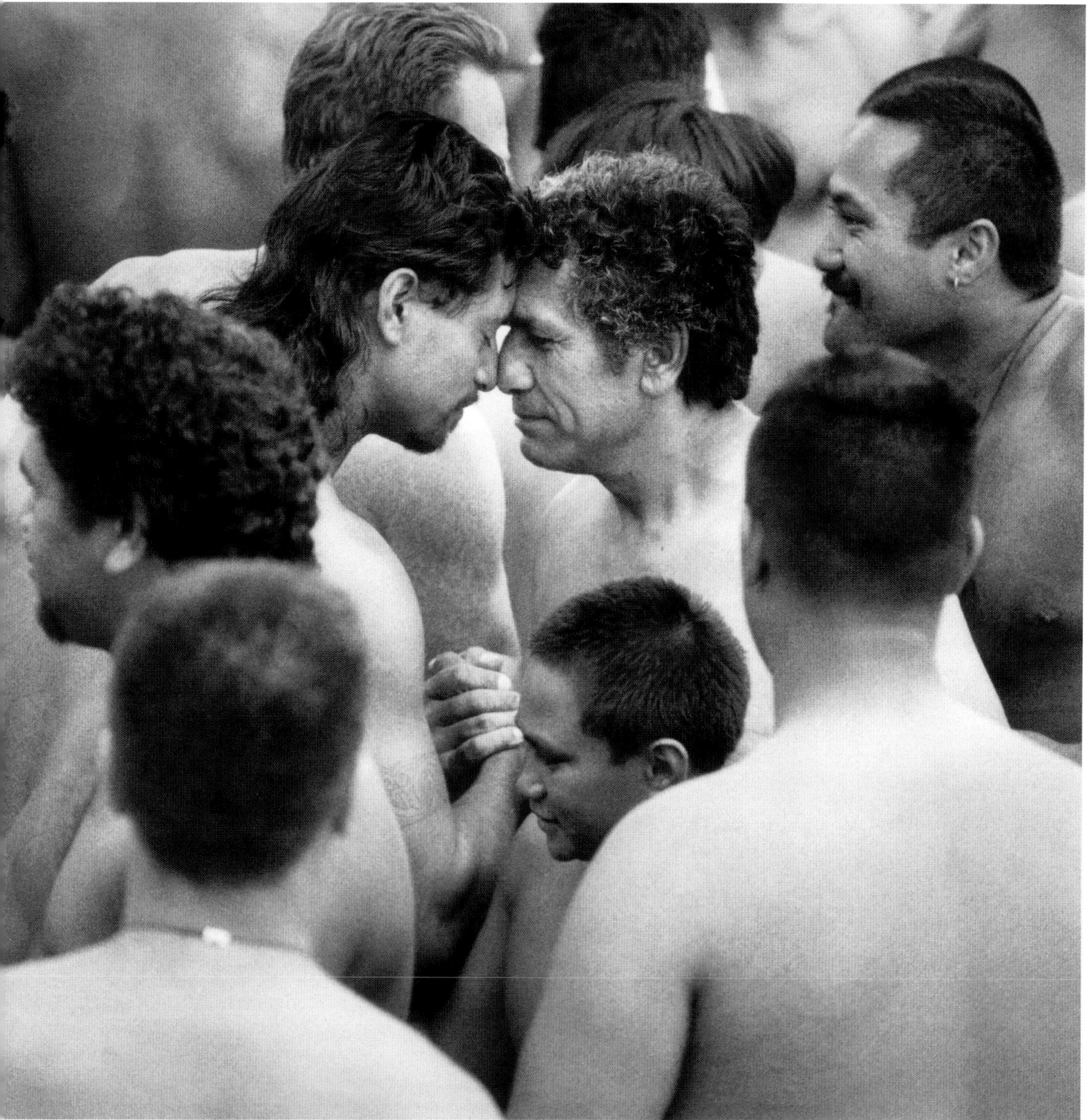

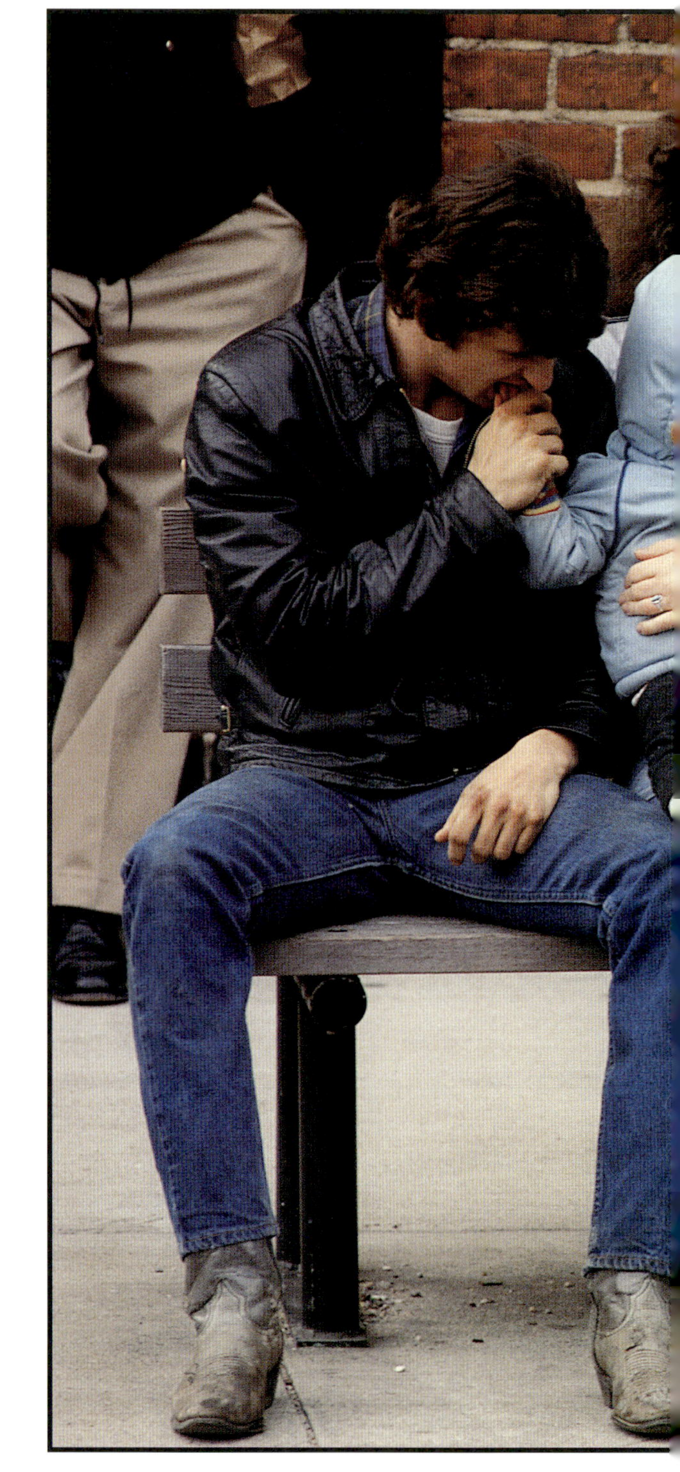

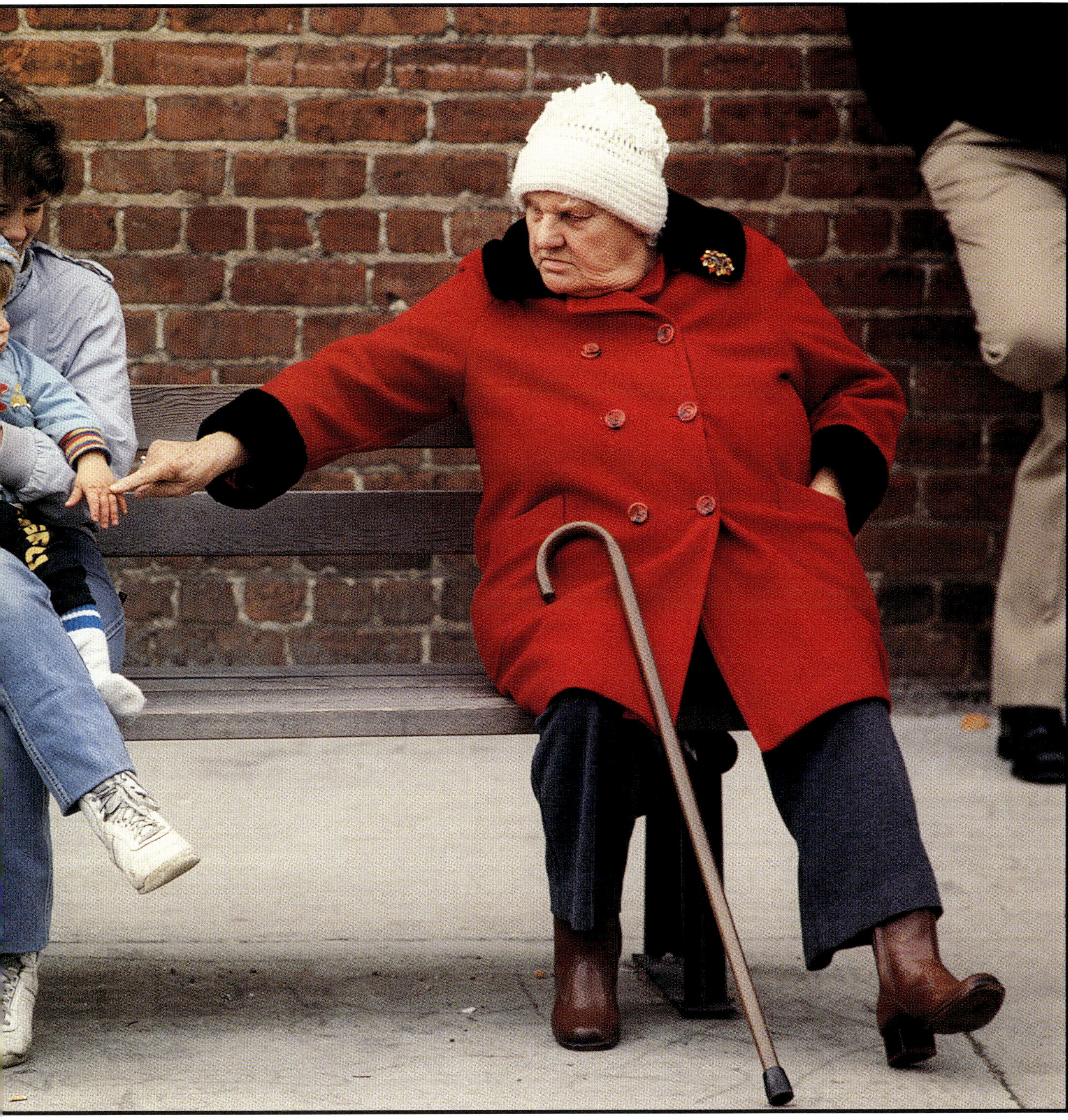

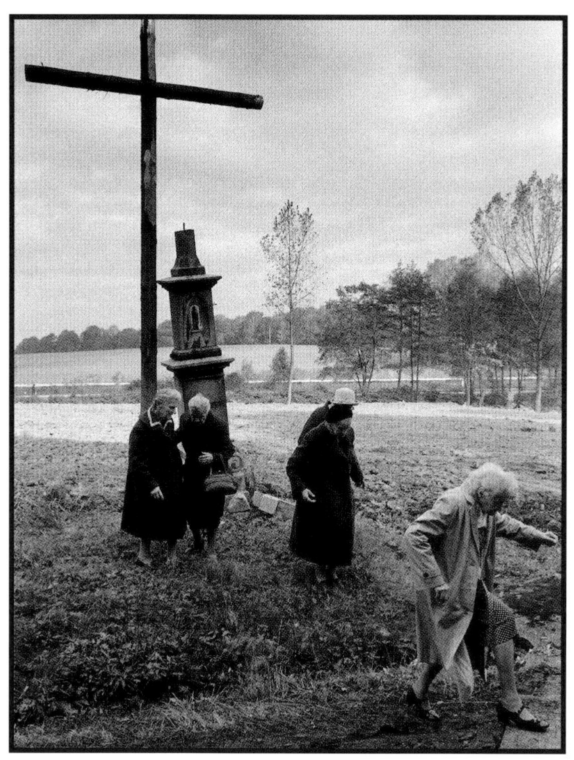

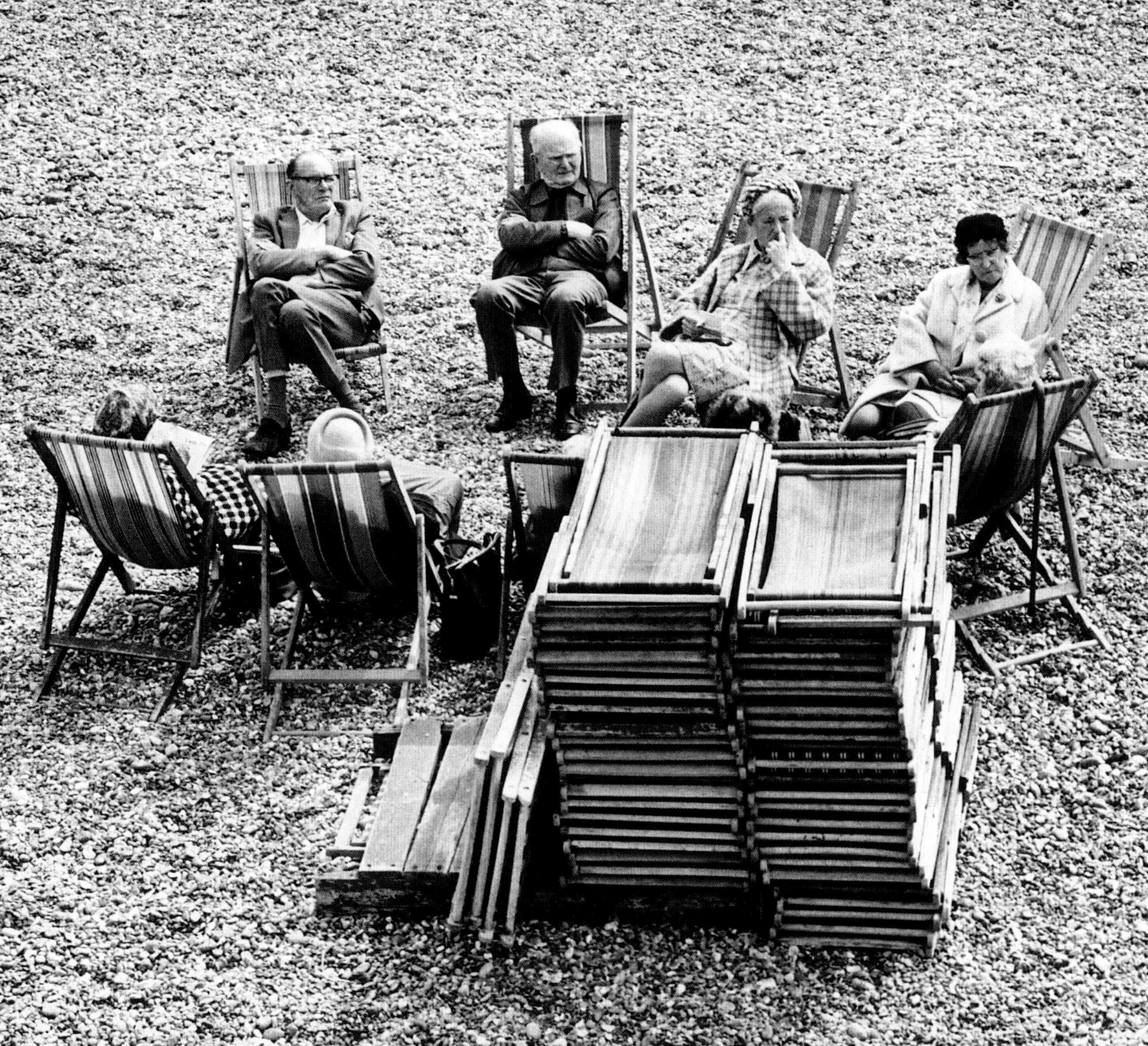

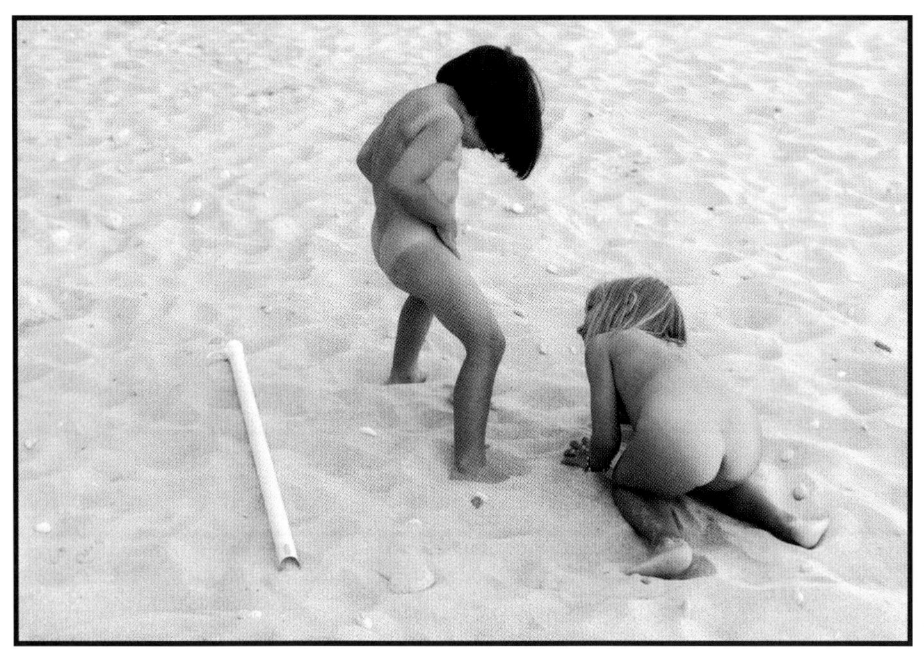

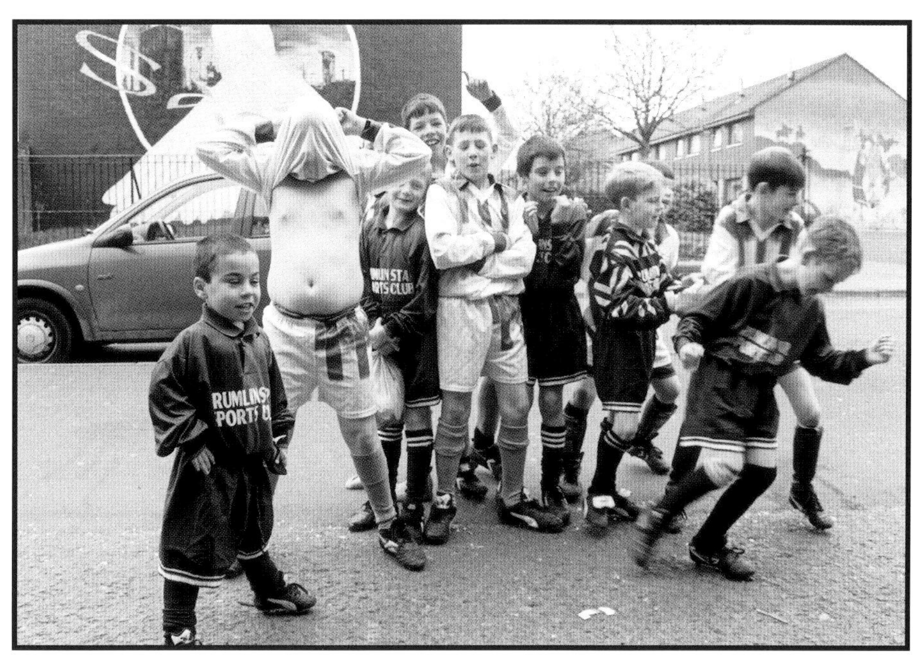

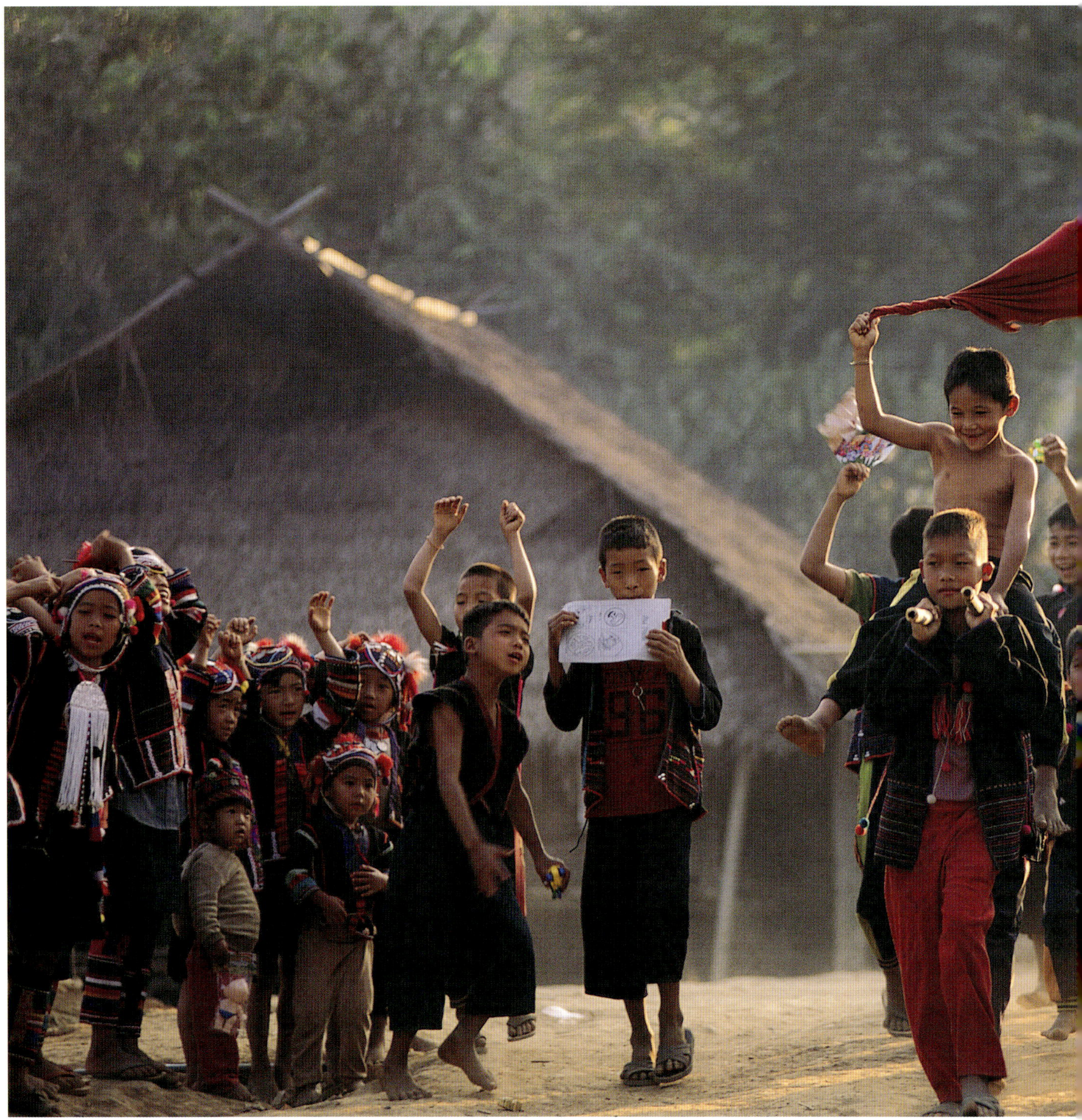

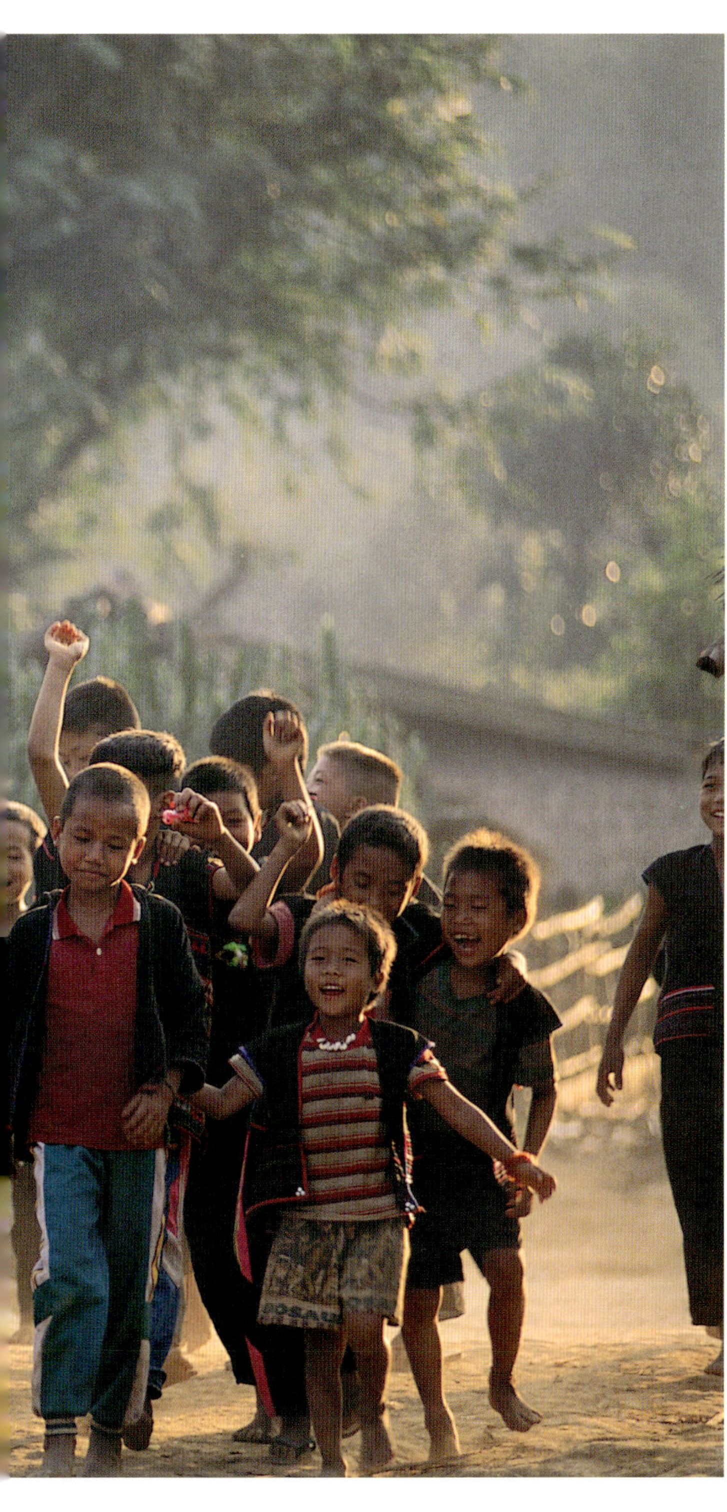

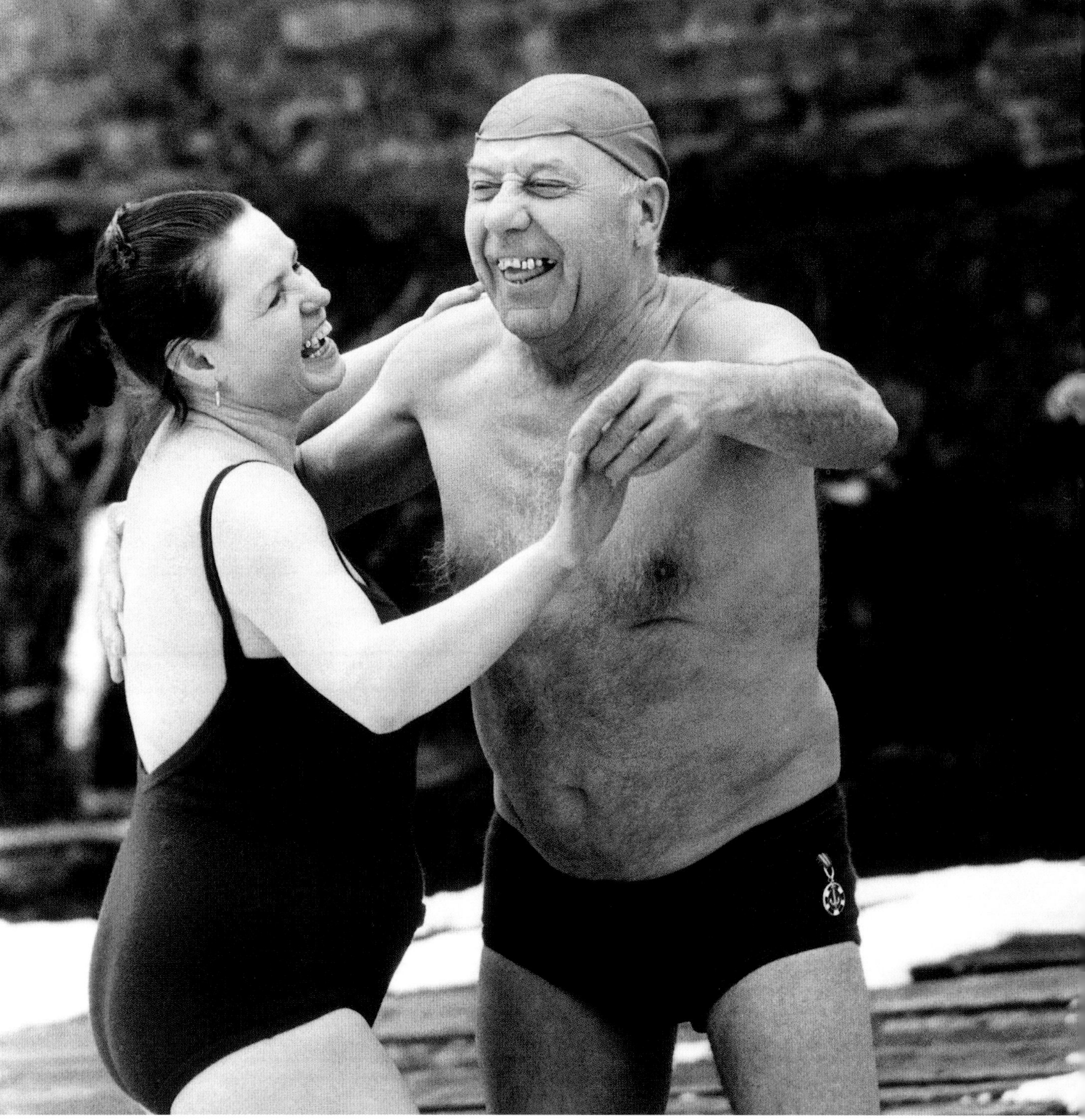

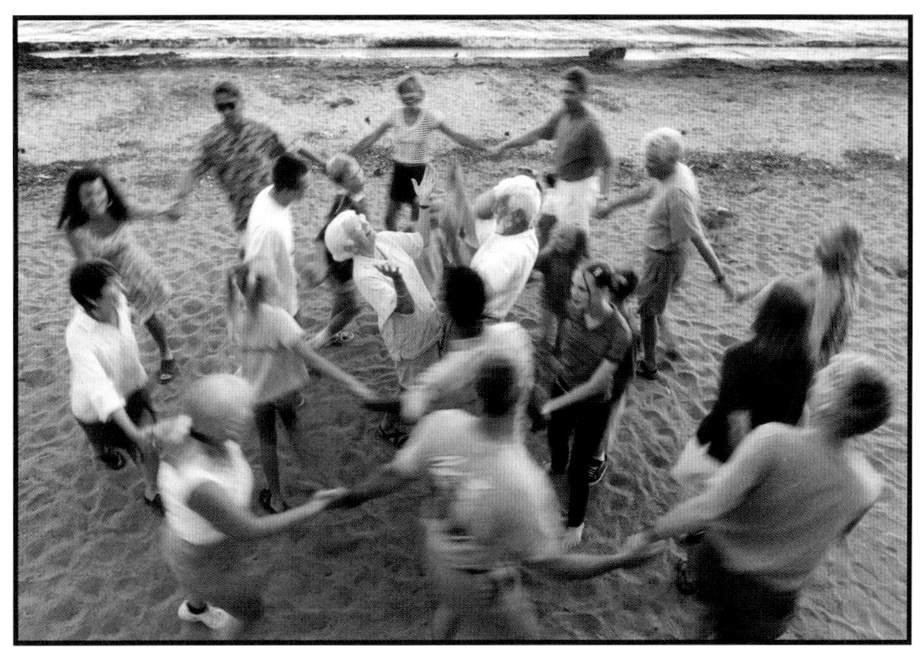

Some people move our souls to dance.

[ANON]

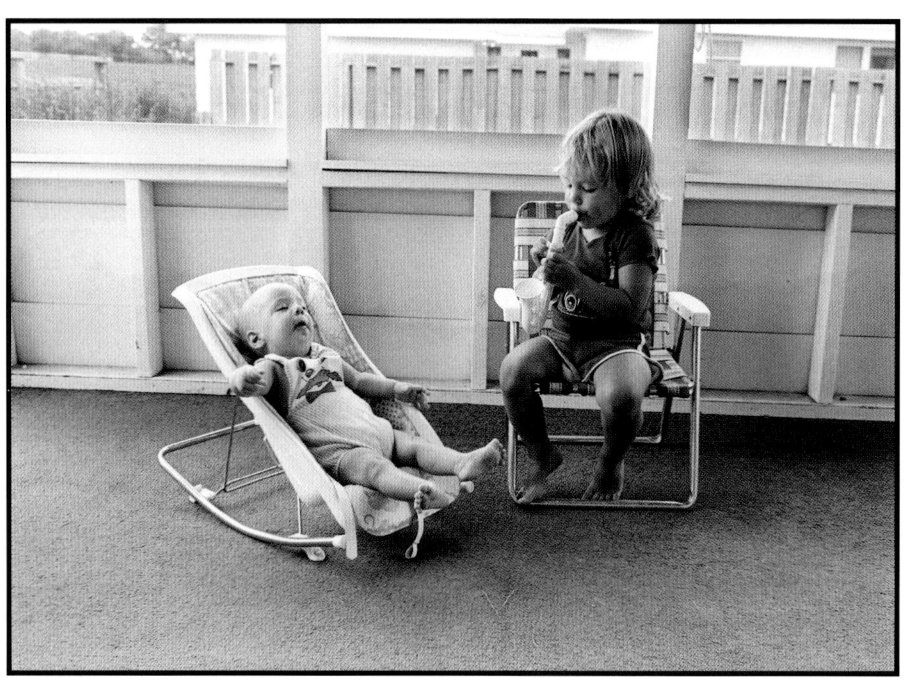

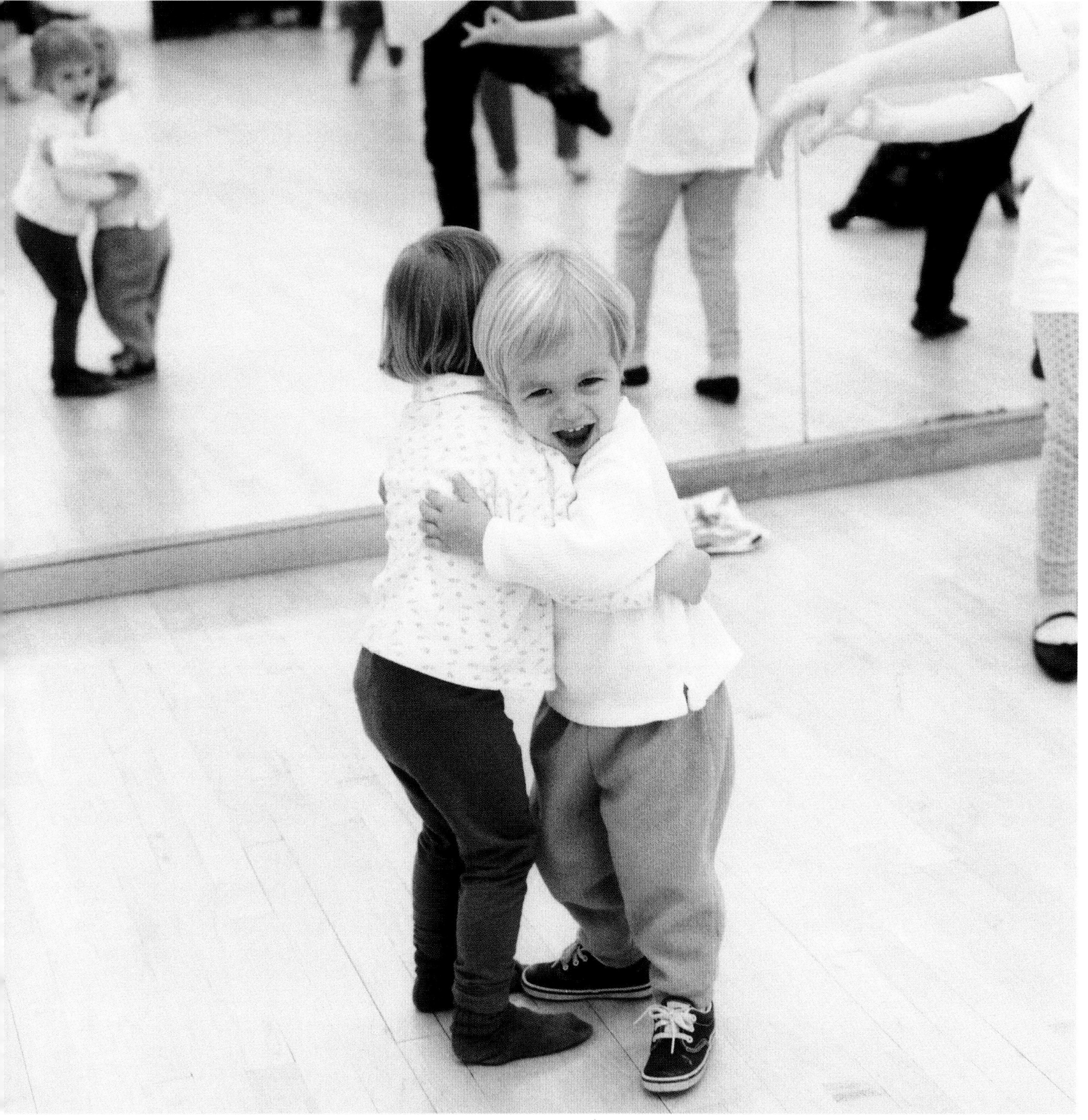

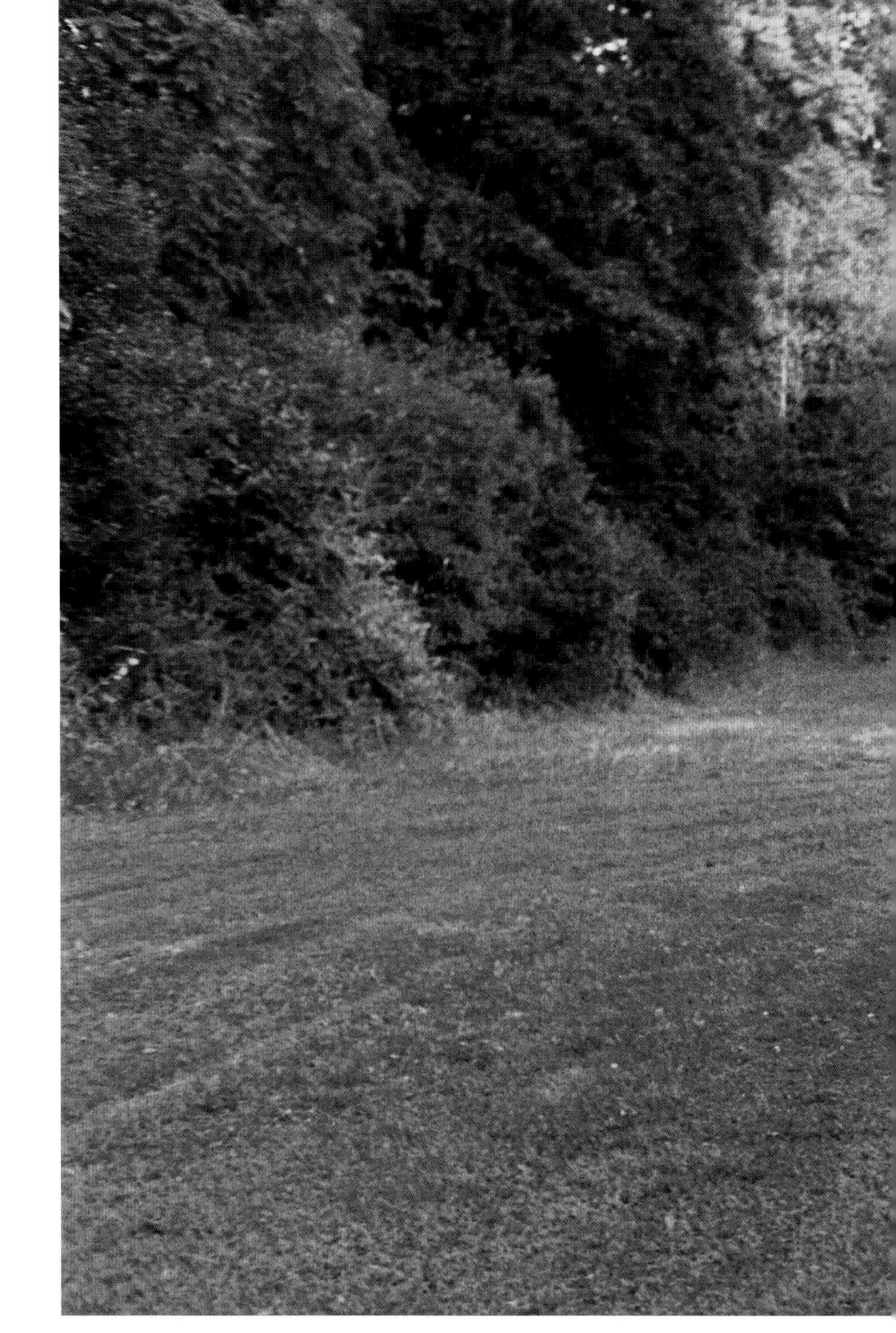

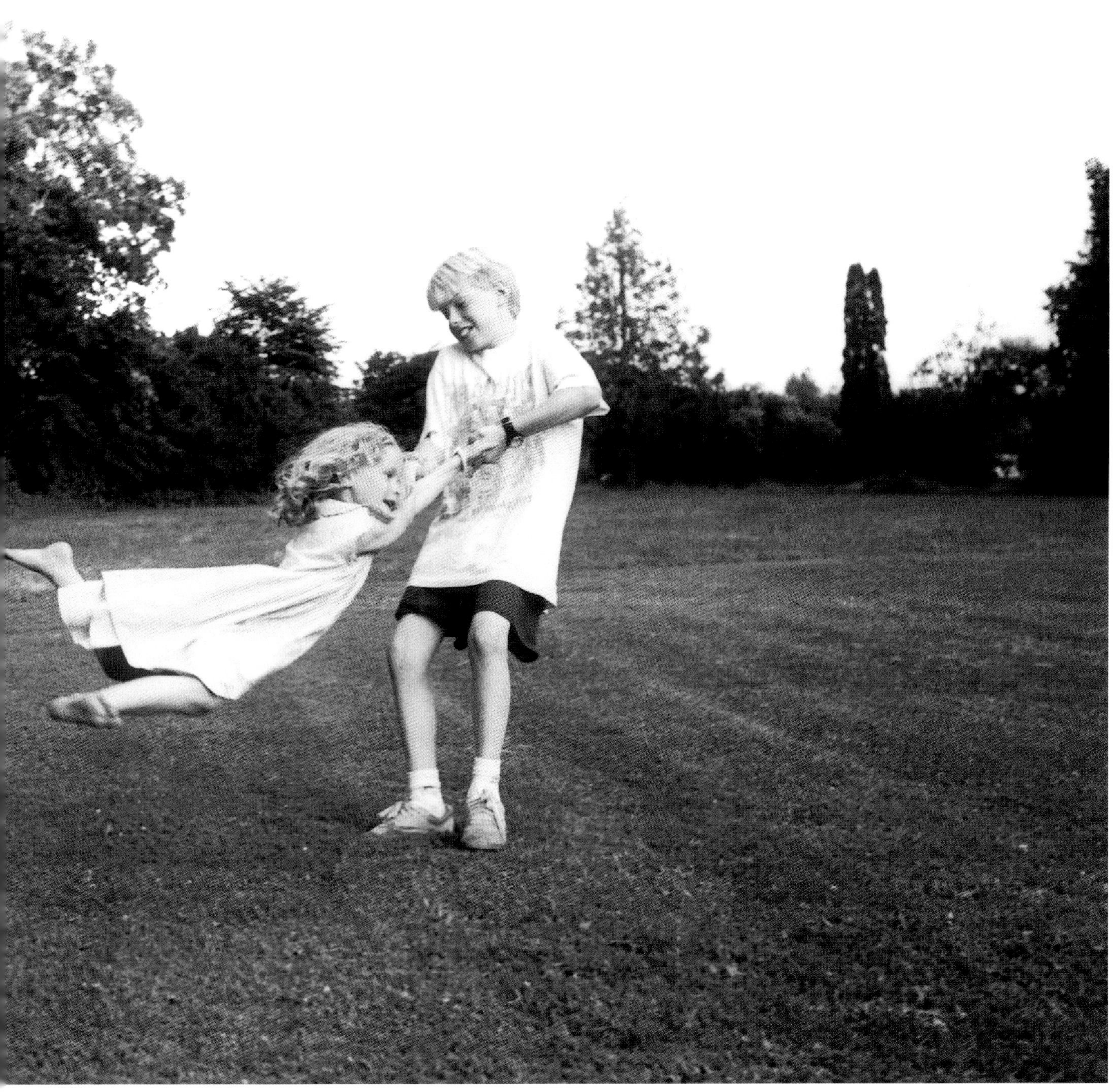

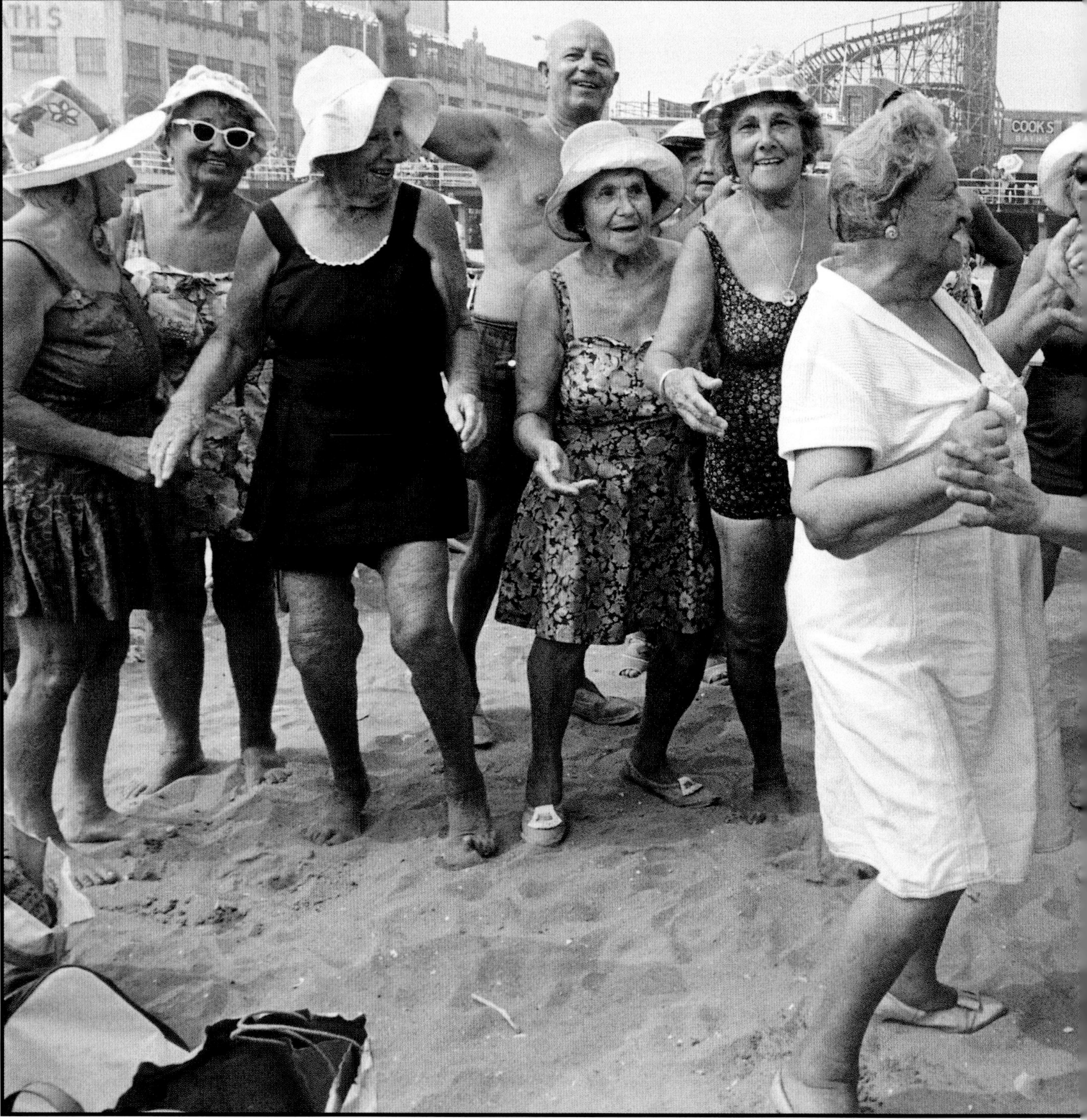
ATHS
COOKS

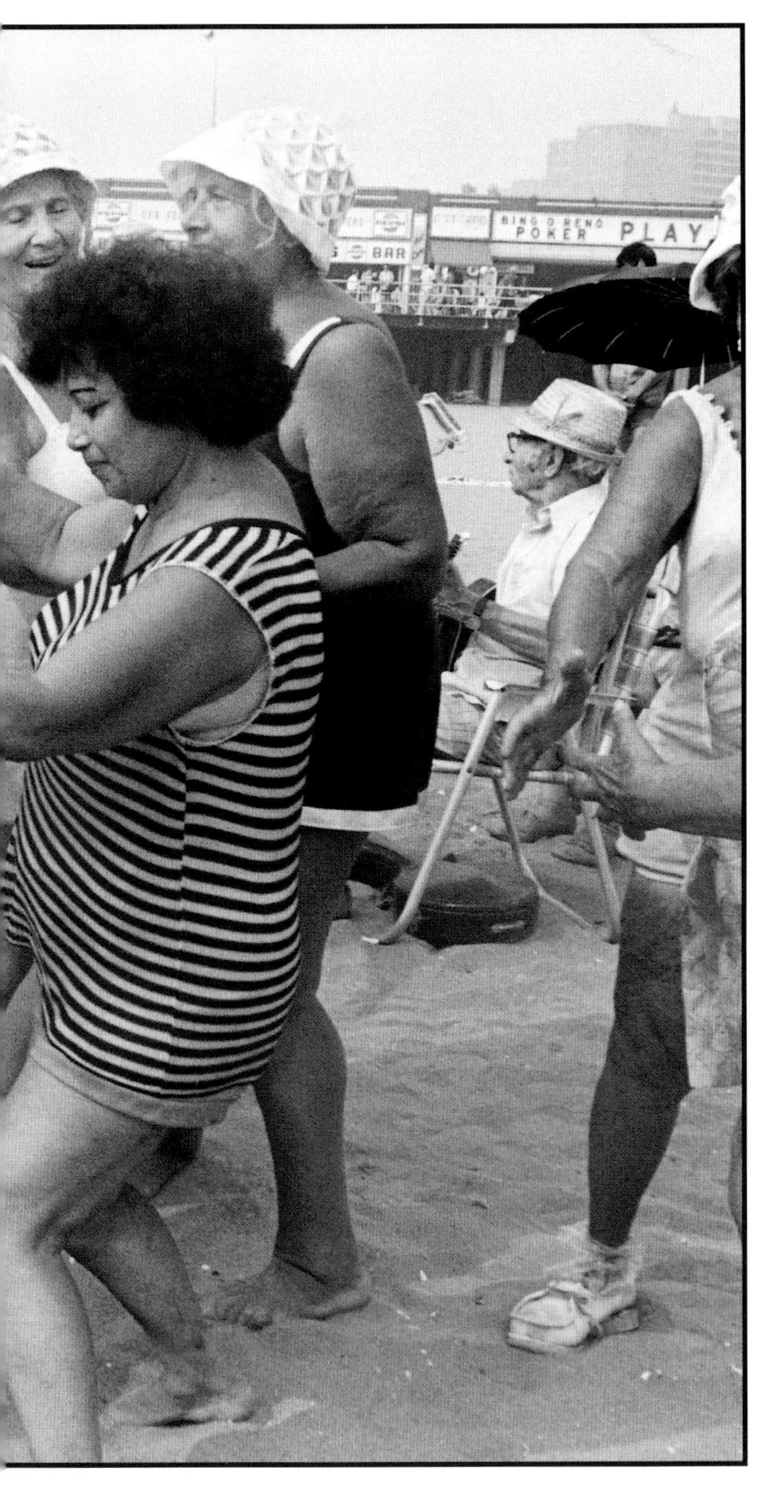
POKER
PLAY
BAR

Real friends are those who, when you've made a fool of yourself,

don't feel that you've done a permanent job.

[ERWIN T. RANDALL]

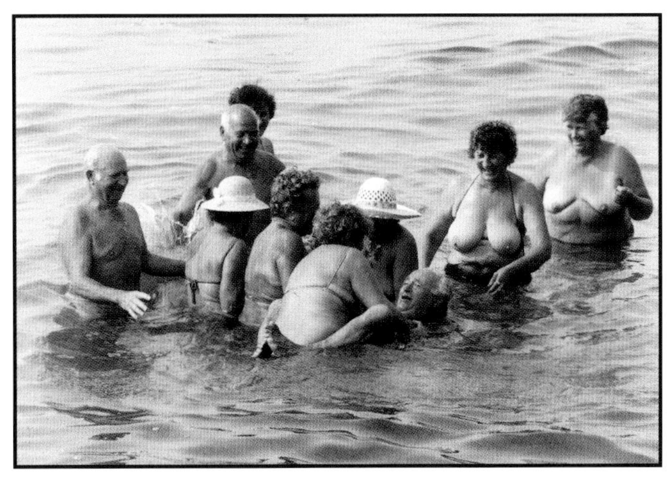

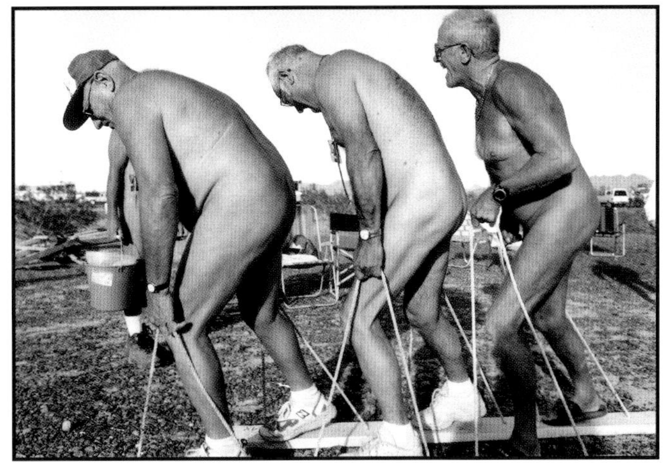

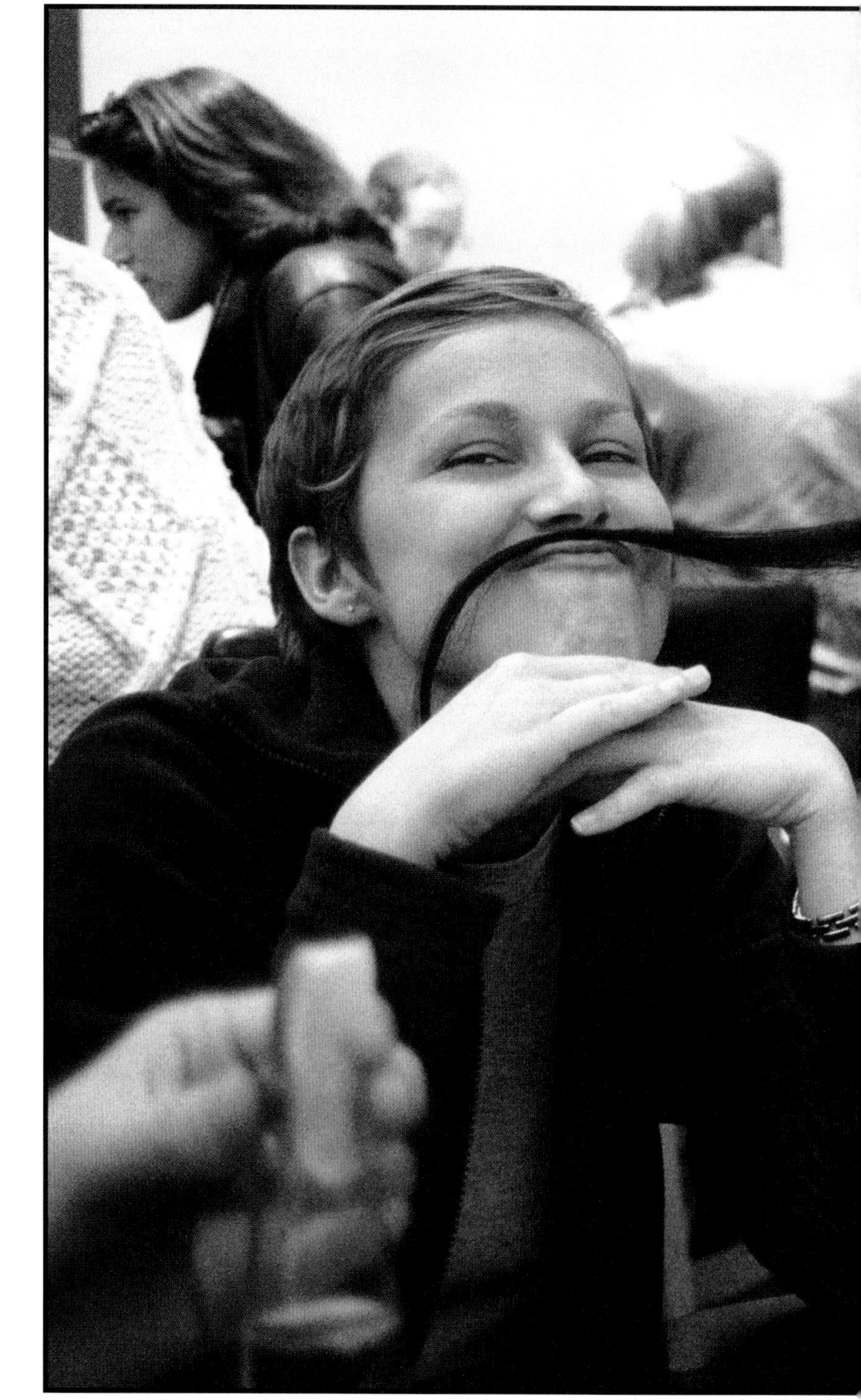

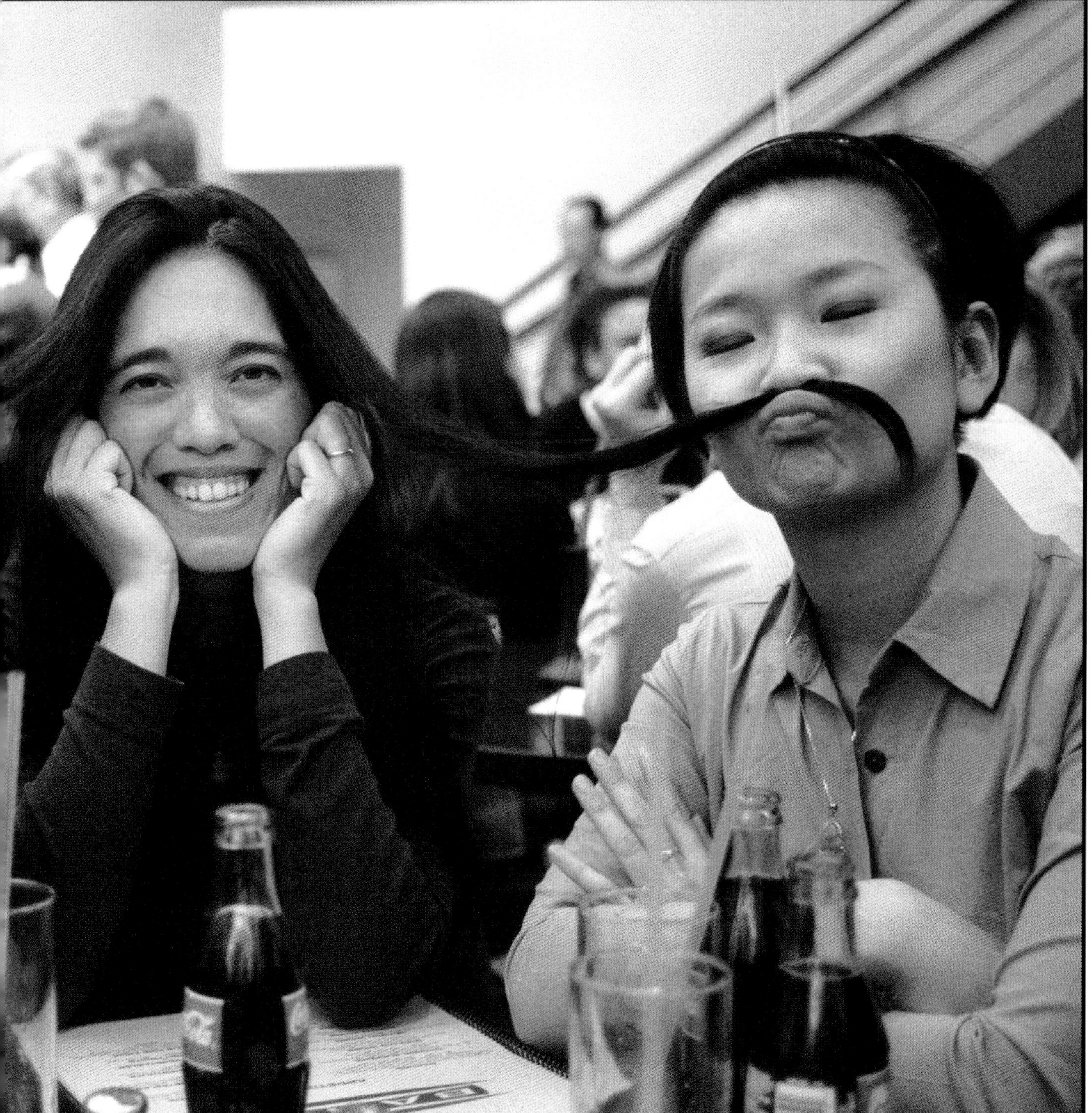

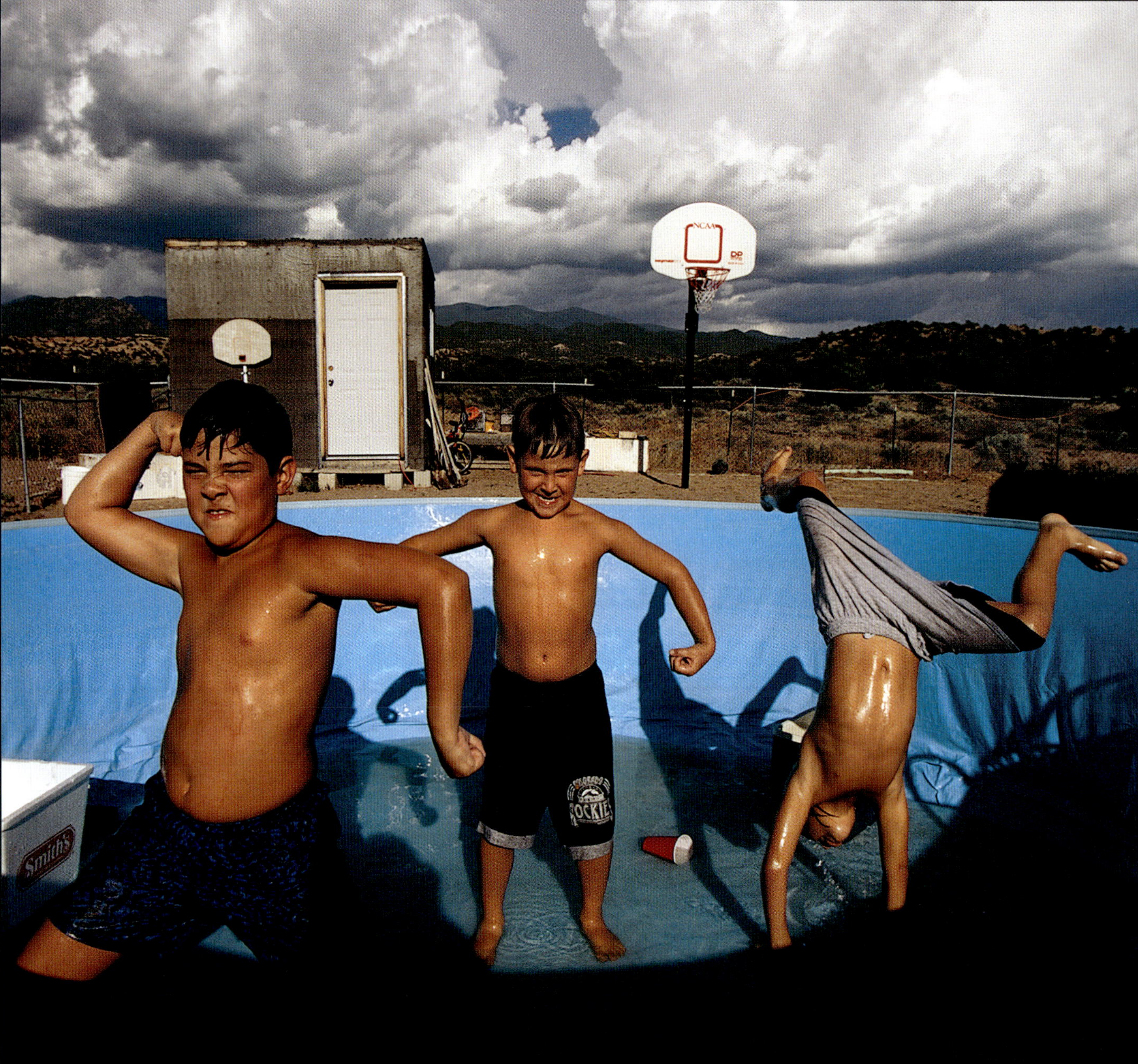
NCAA
Smith's

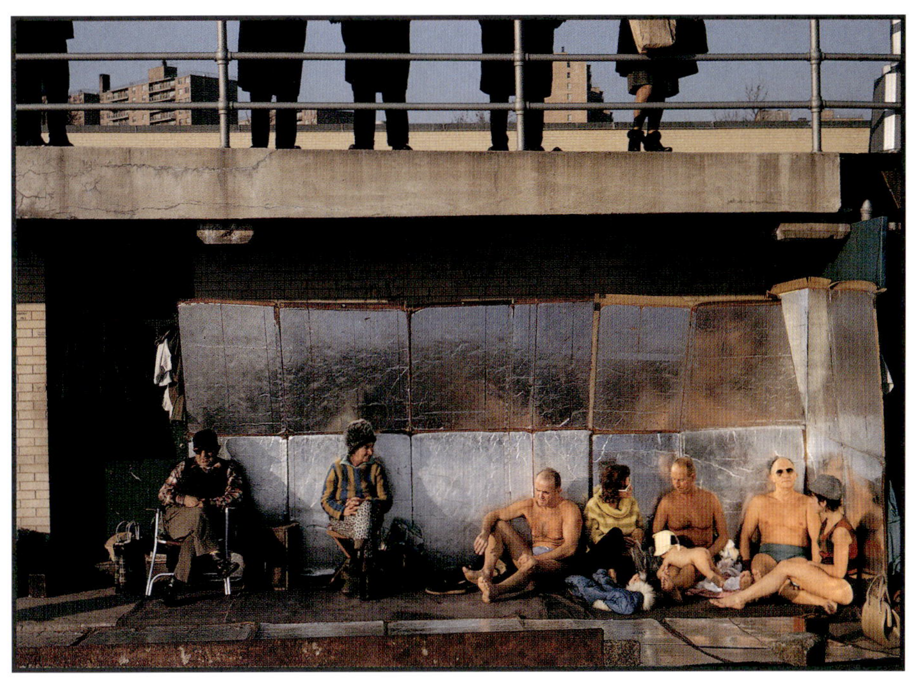

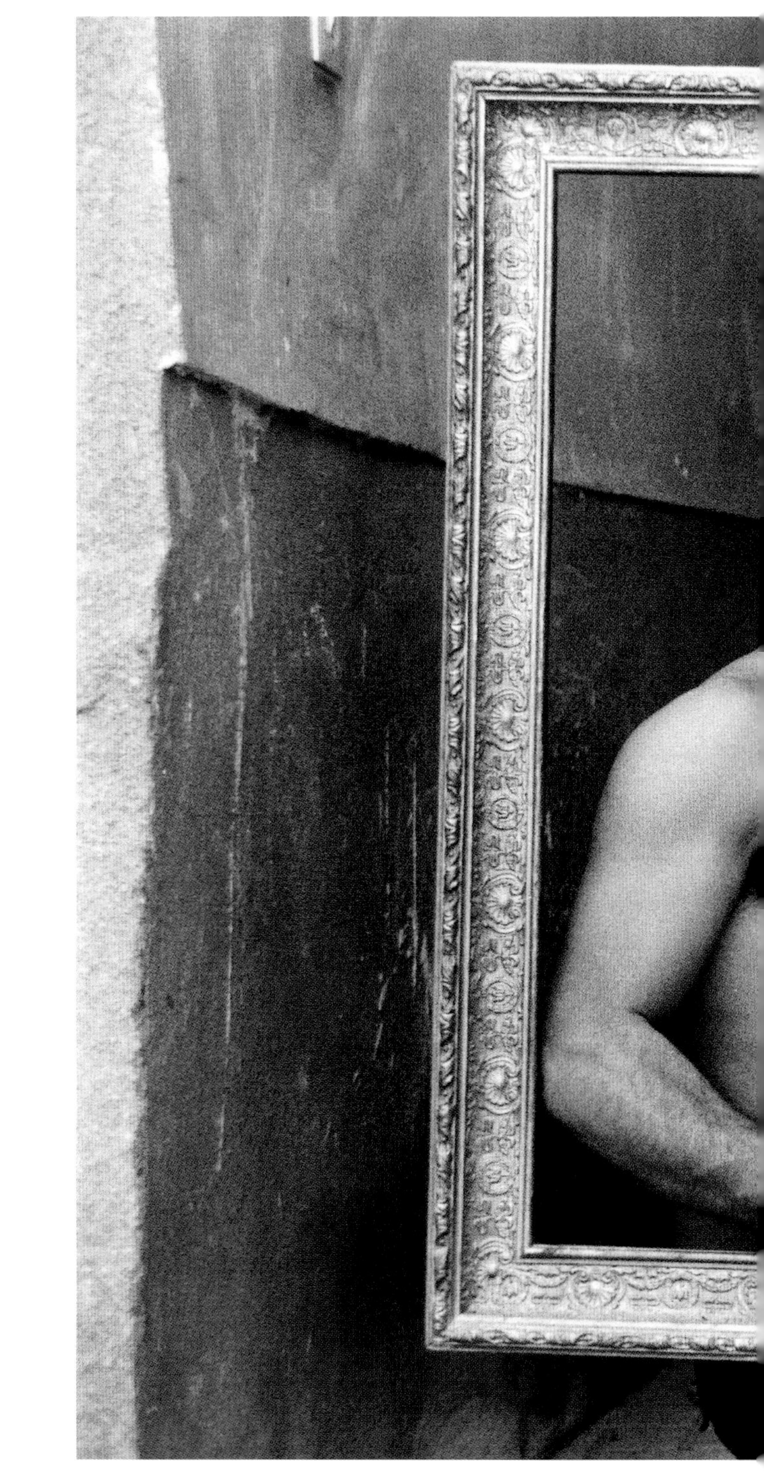

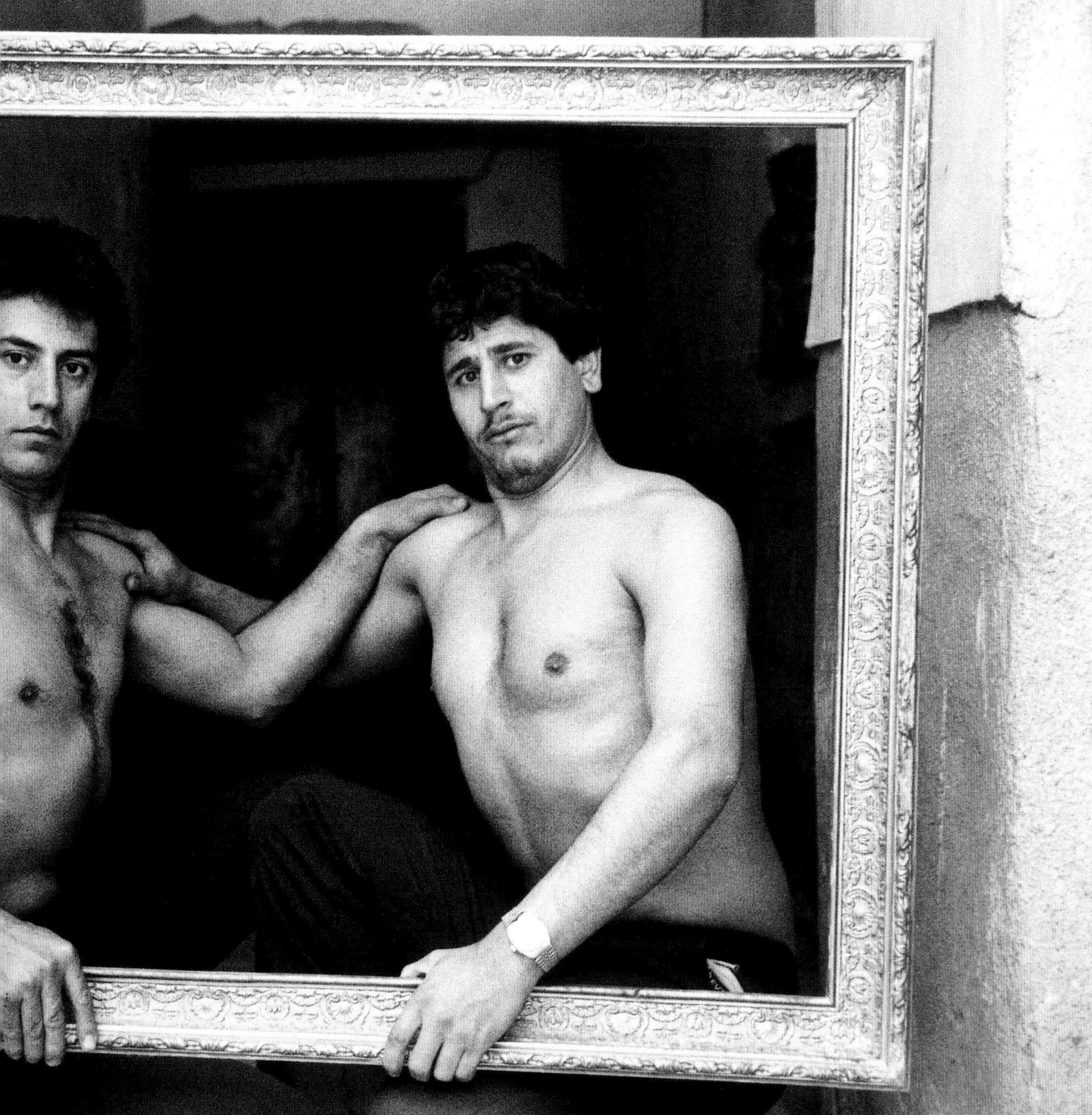

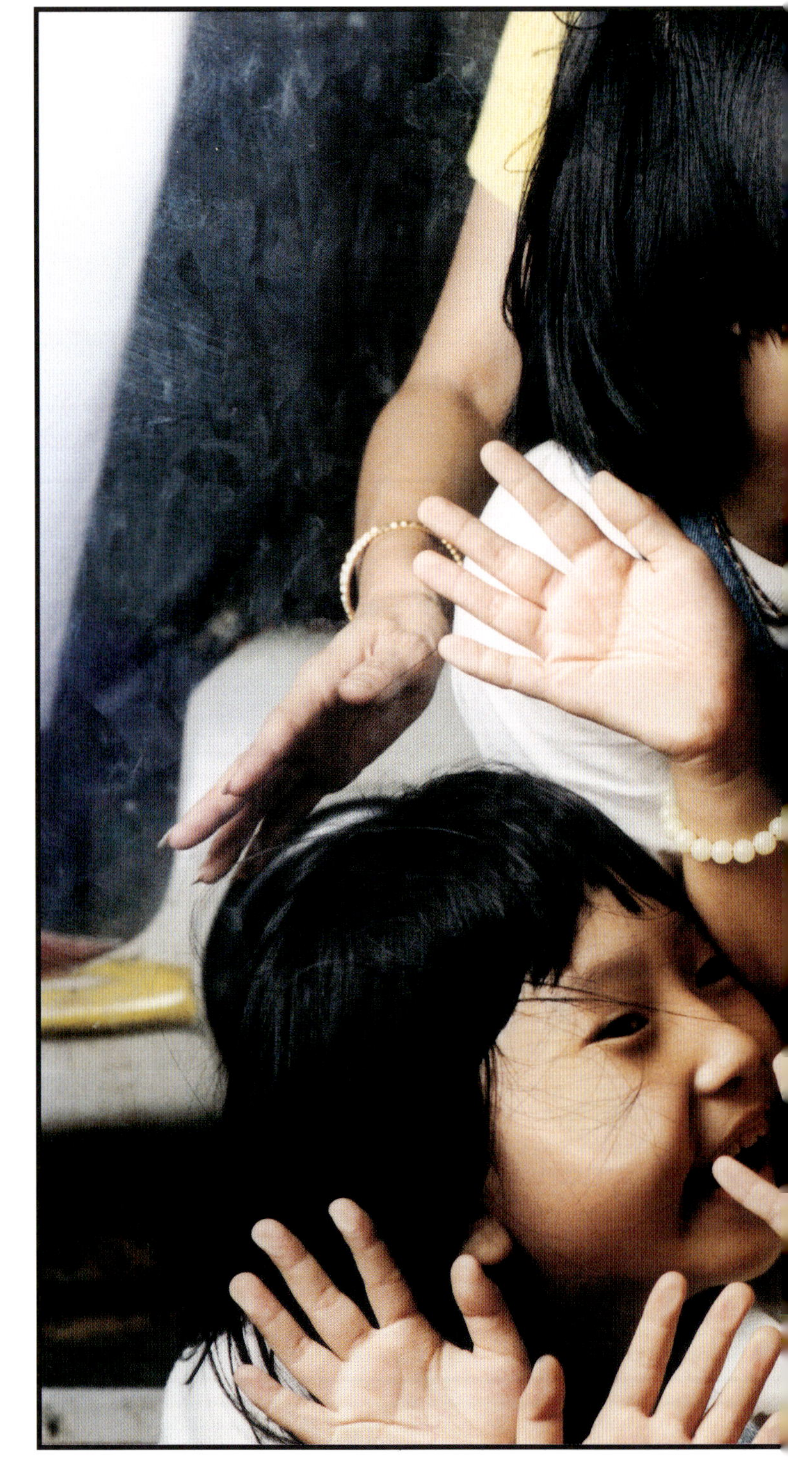

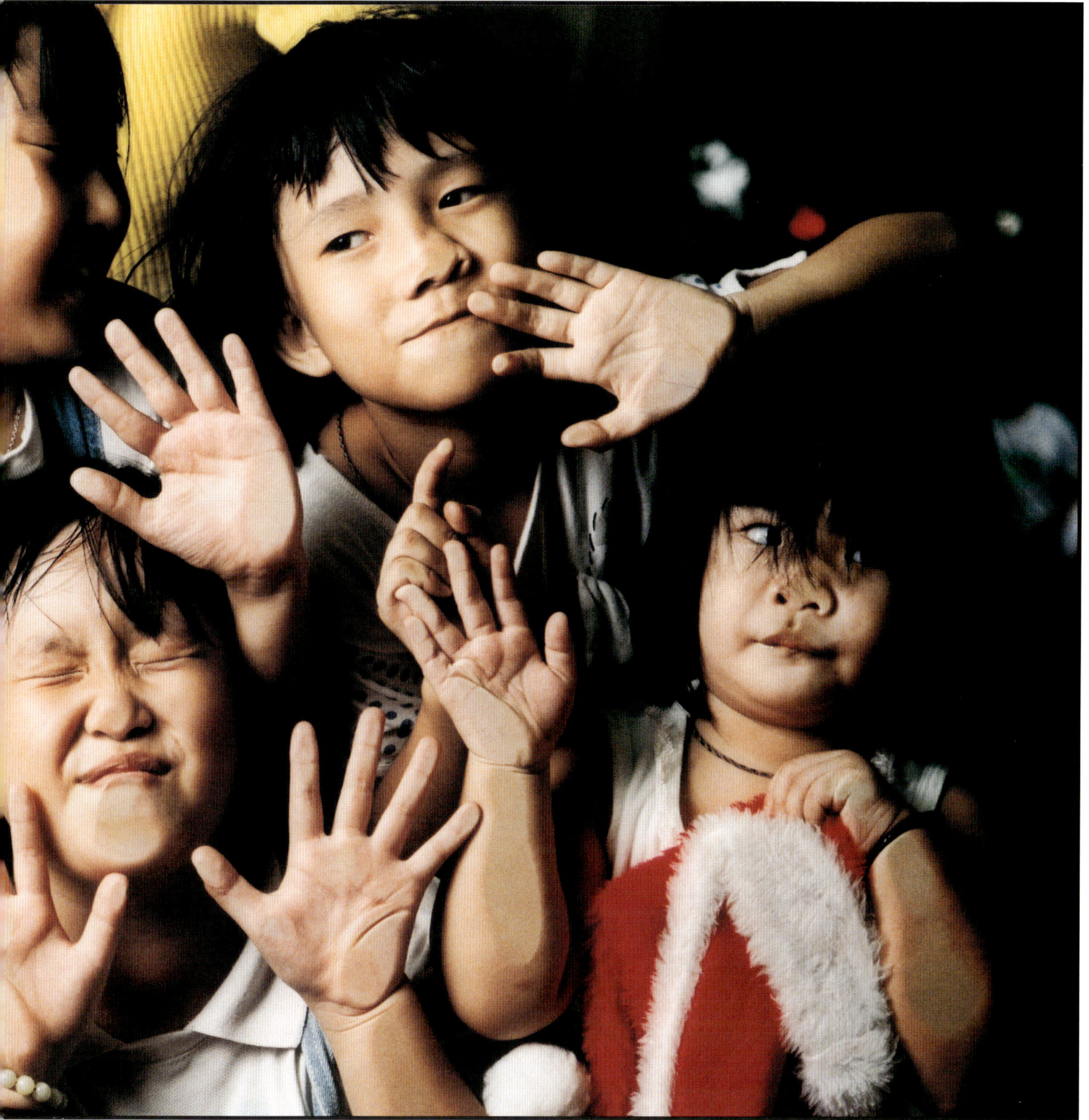

Laughter is the shortest distance between **two people**.

[ERWIN T. RANDALL]

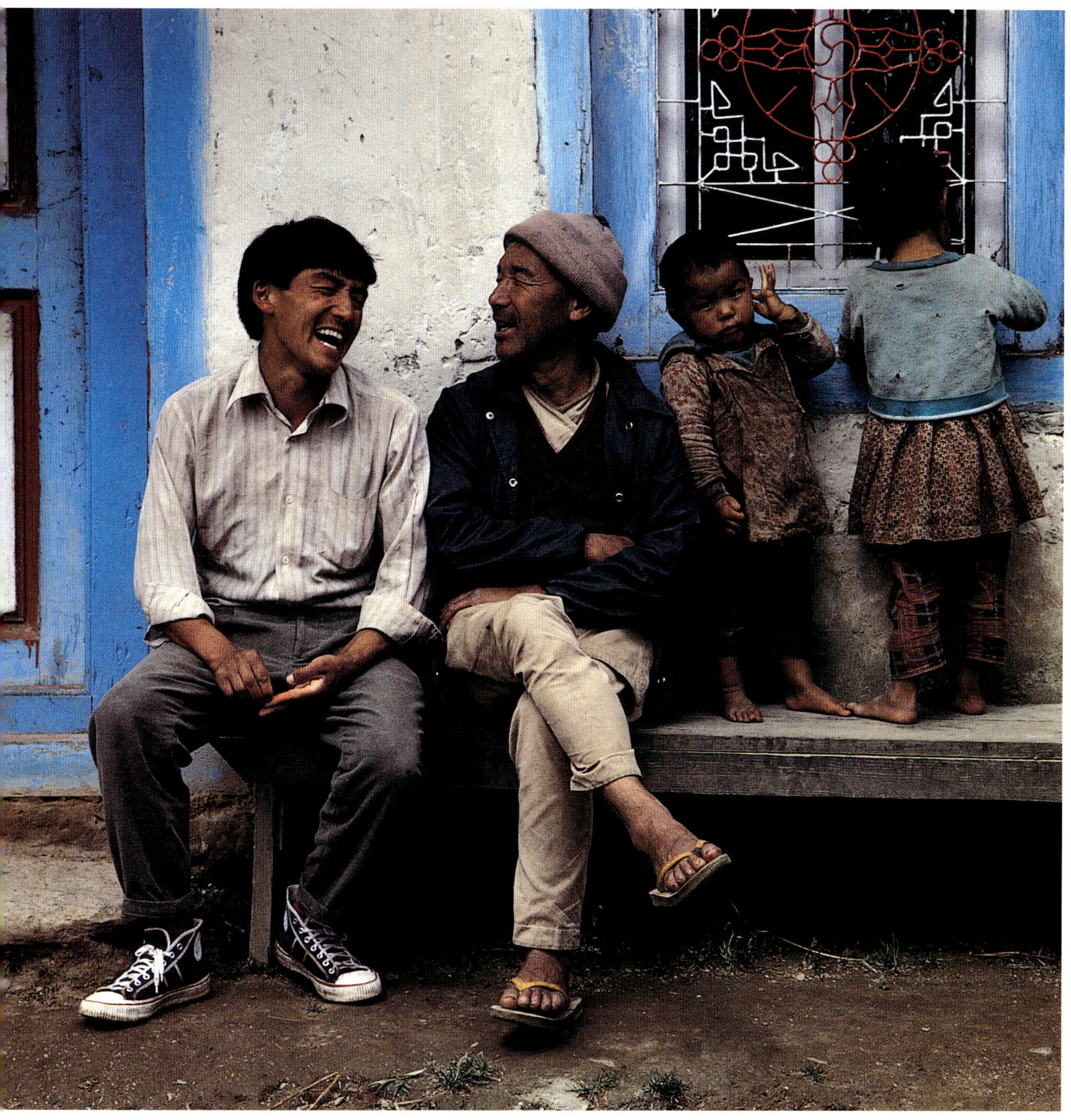

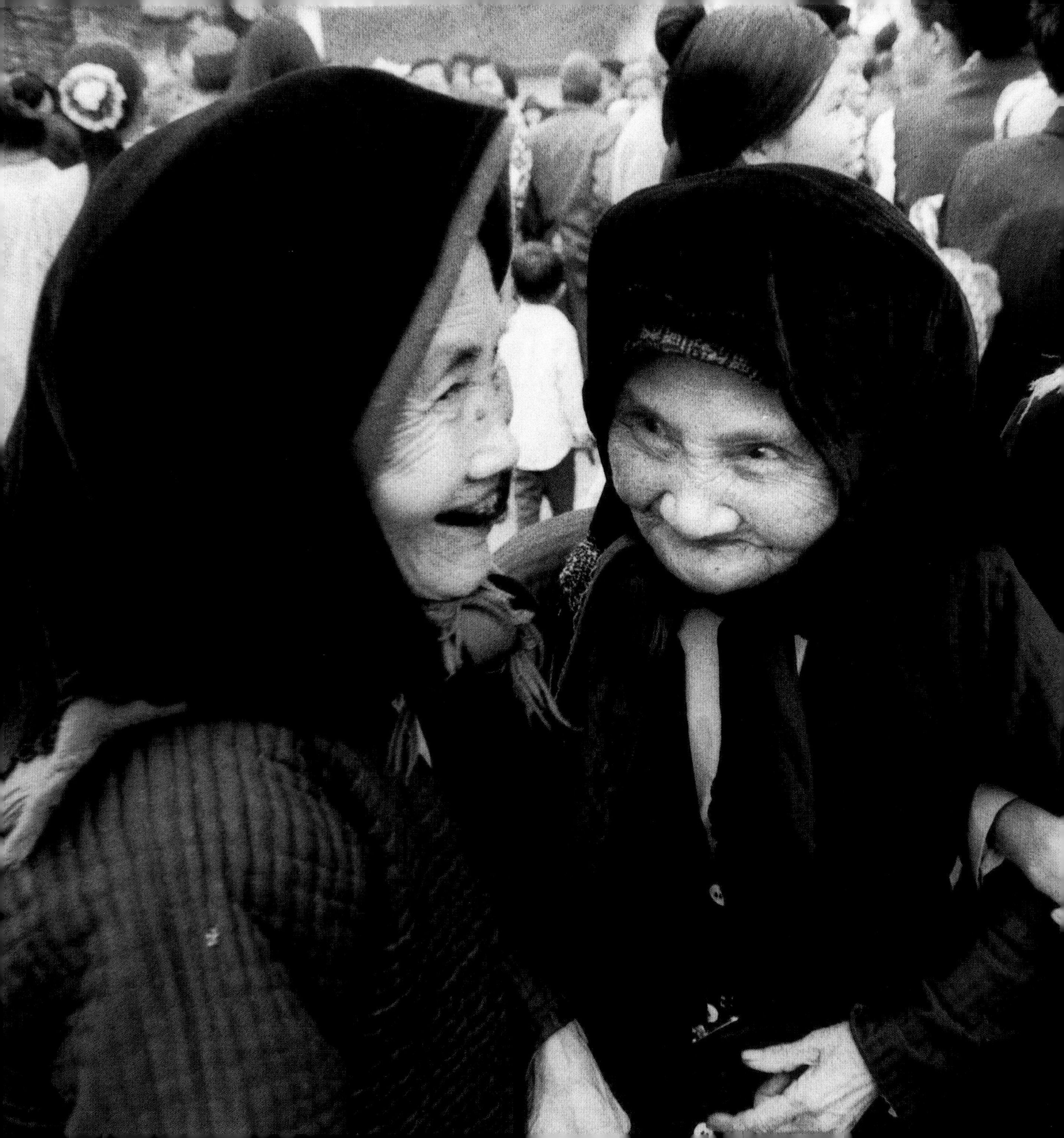

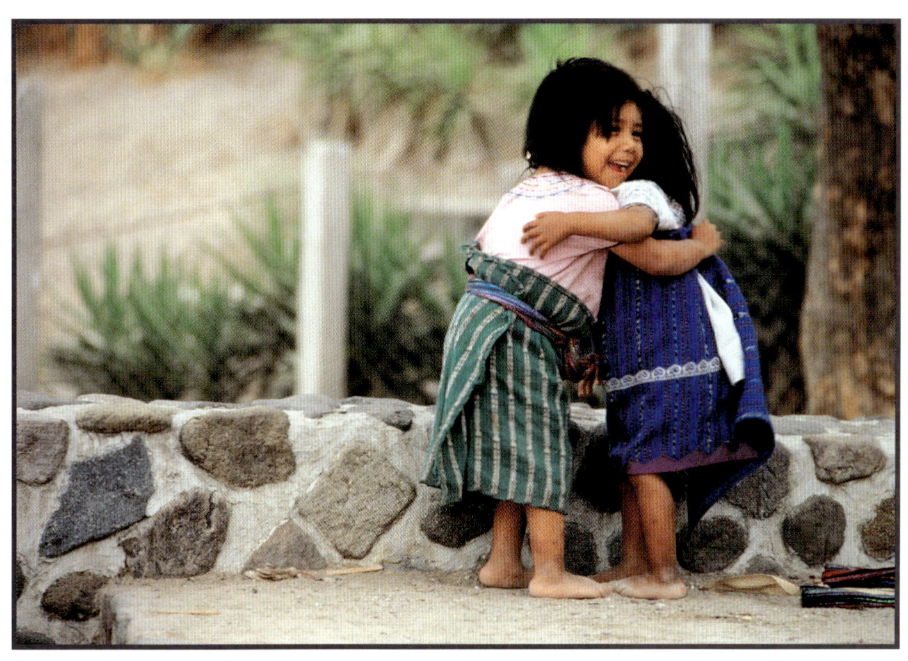

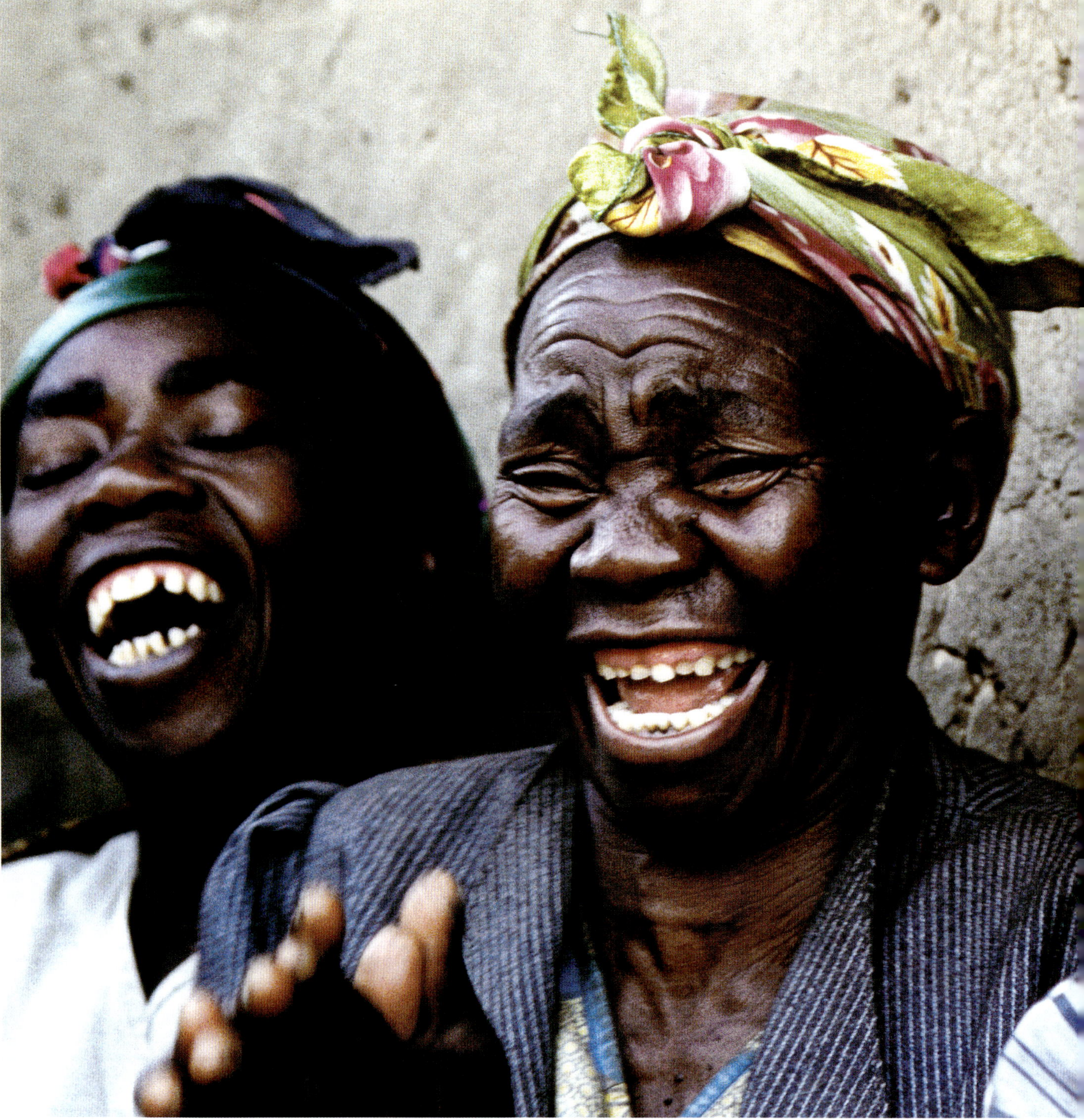

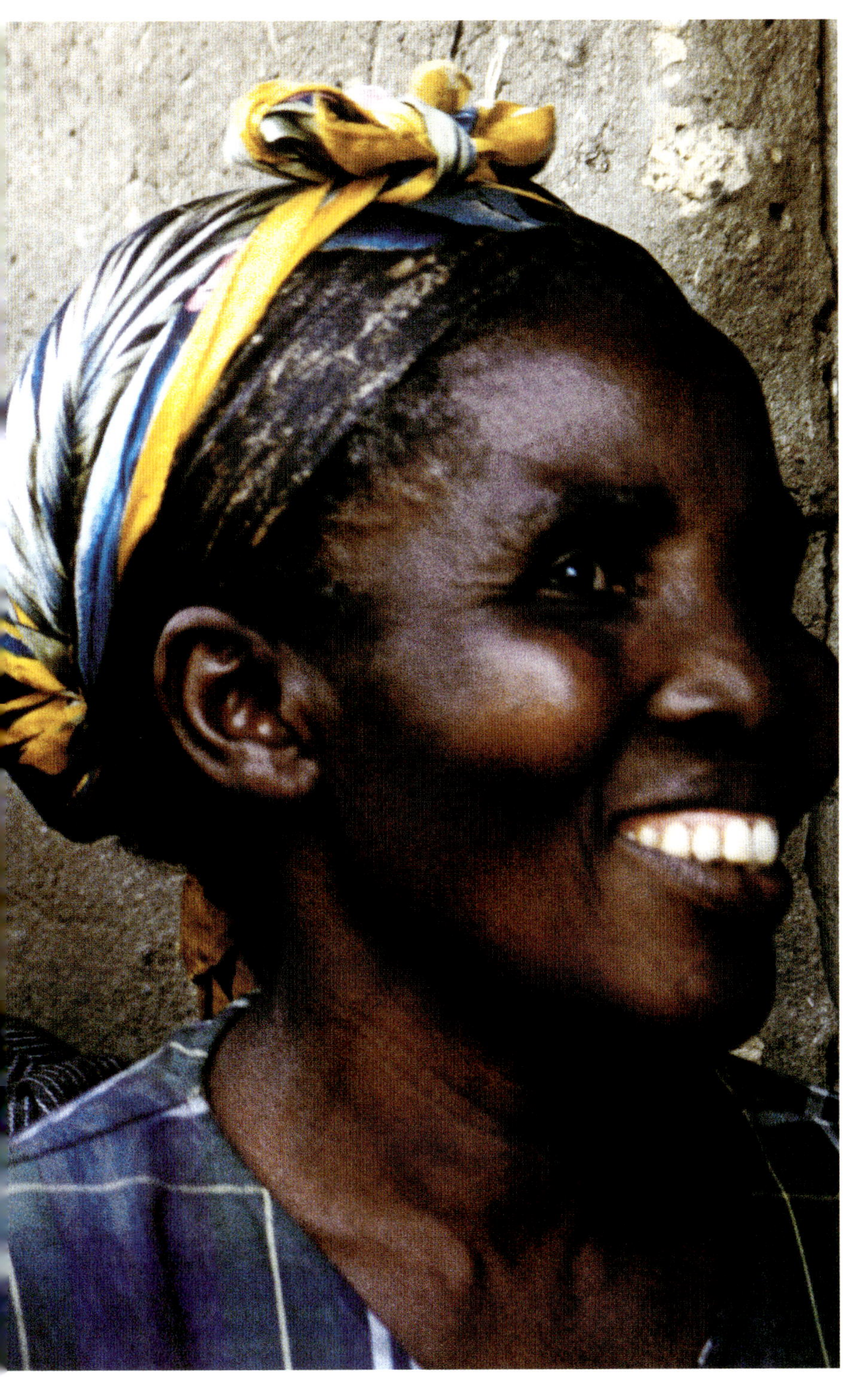

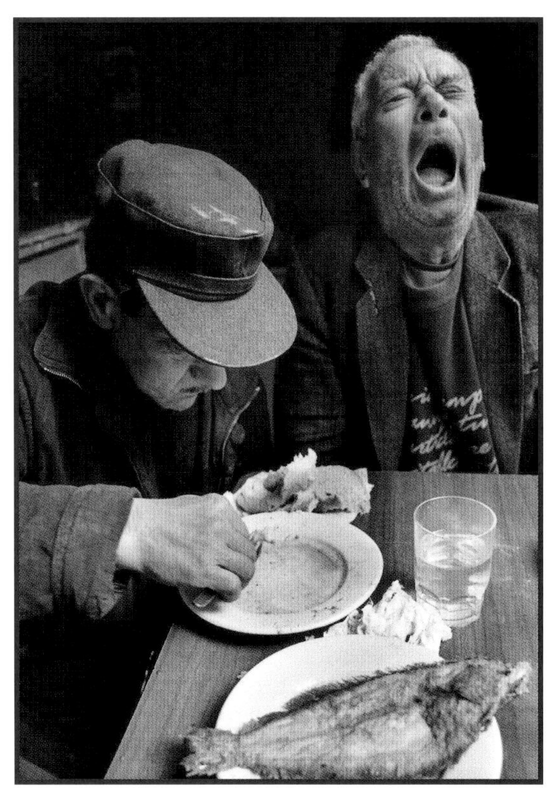

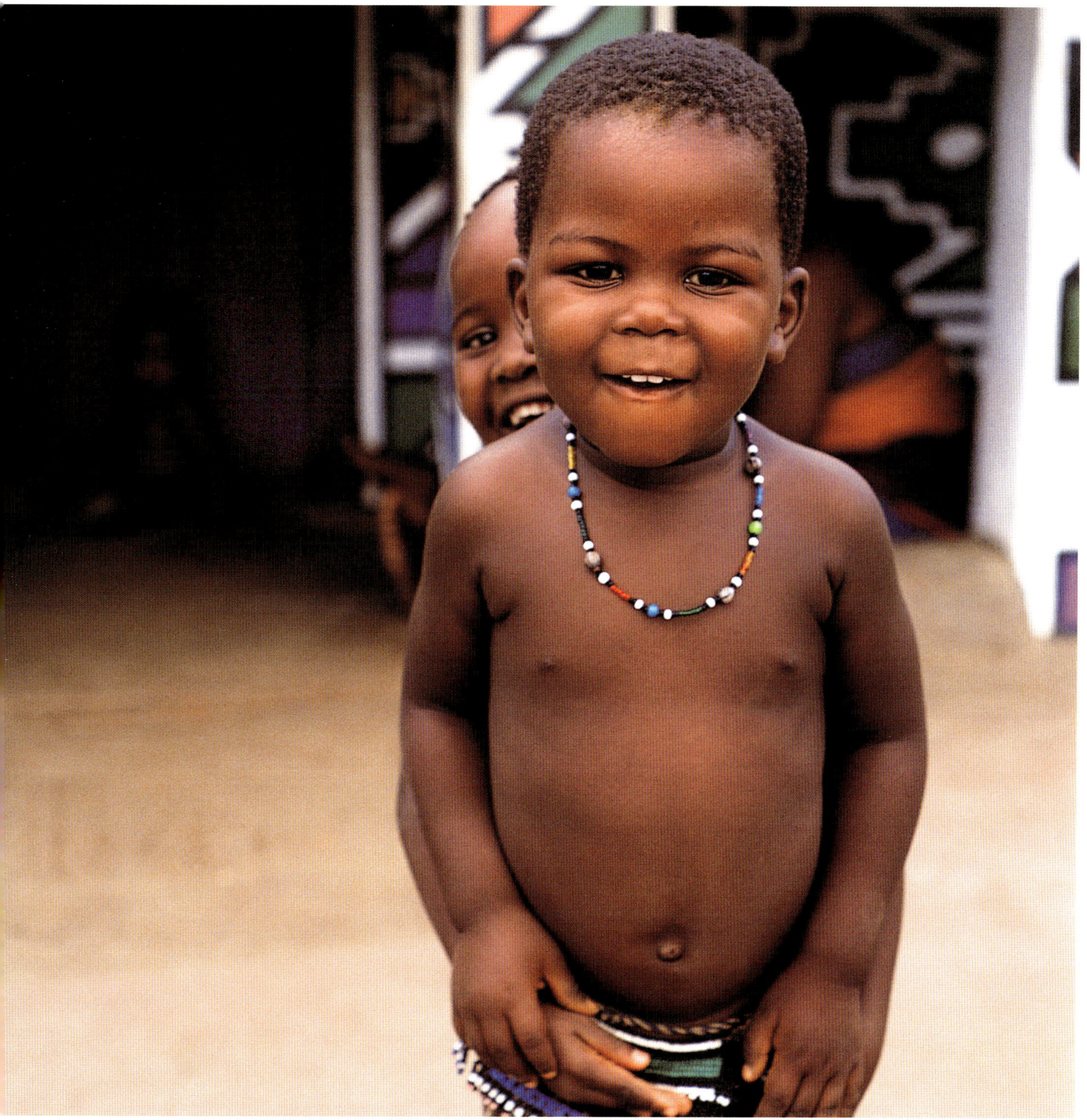

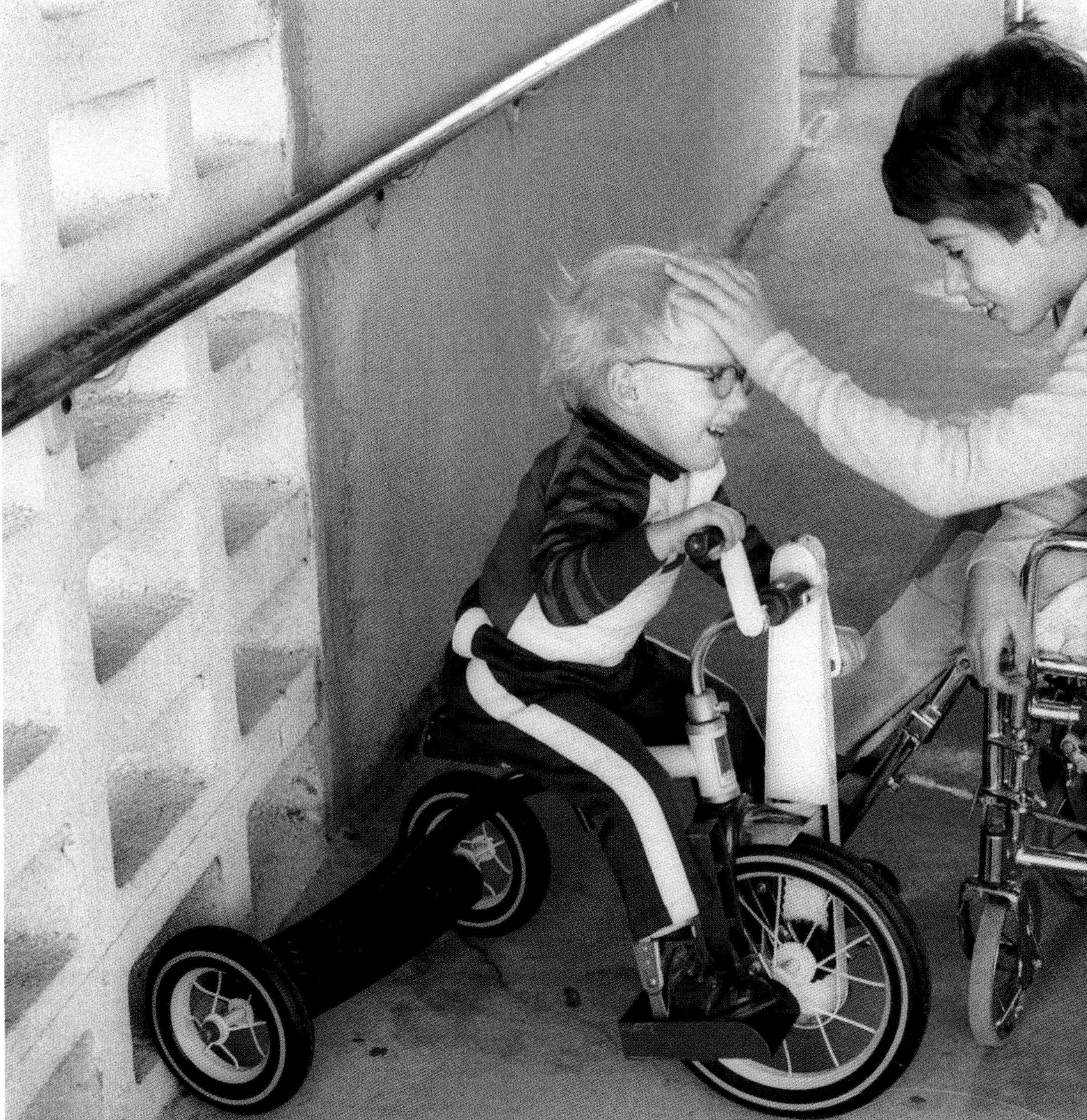

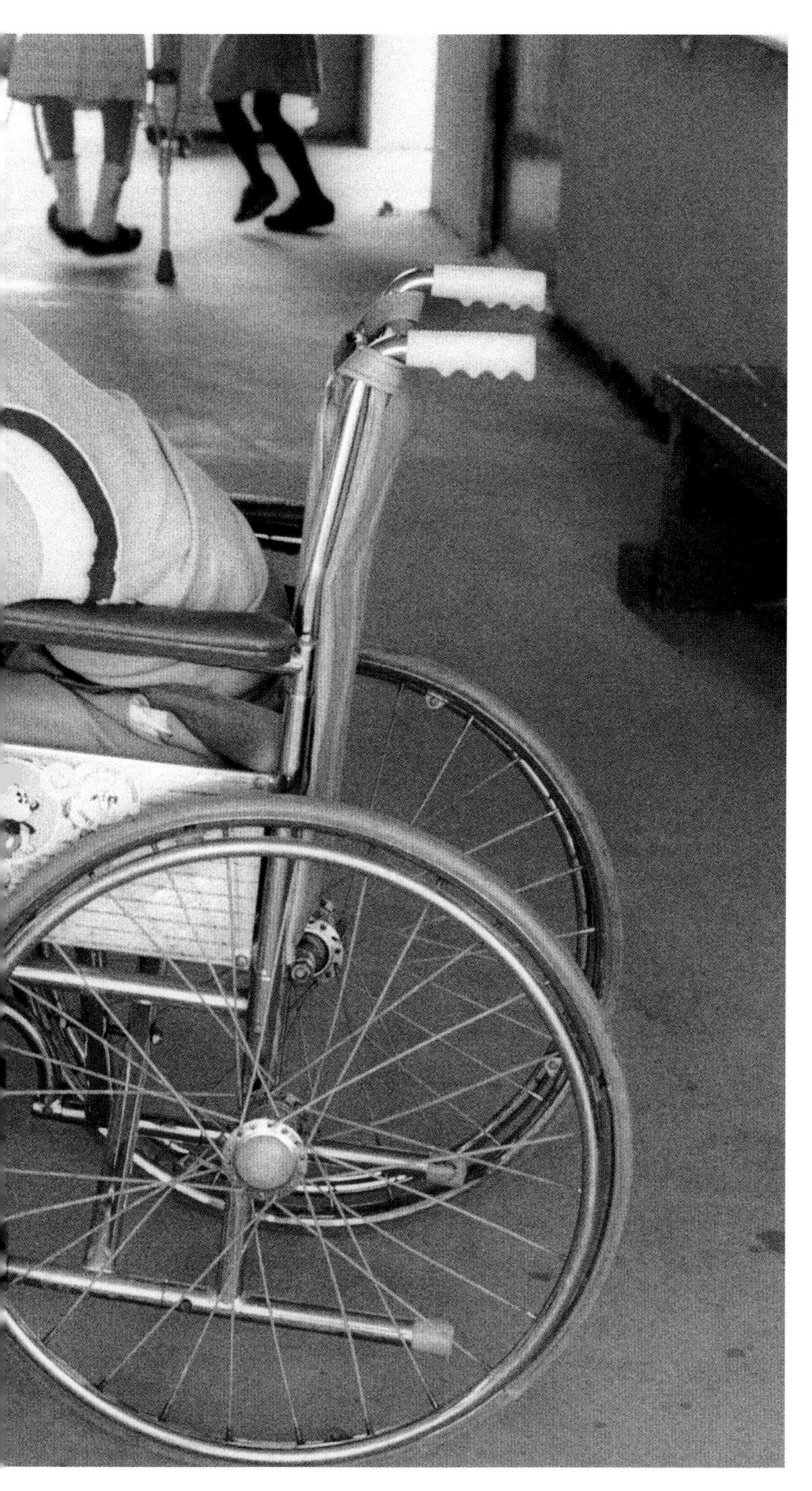

The road to a friend's house is never long.

[DANISH PROVERB]

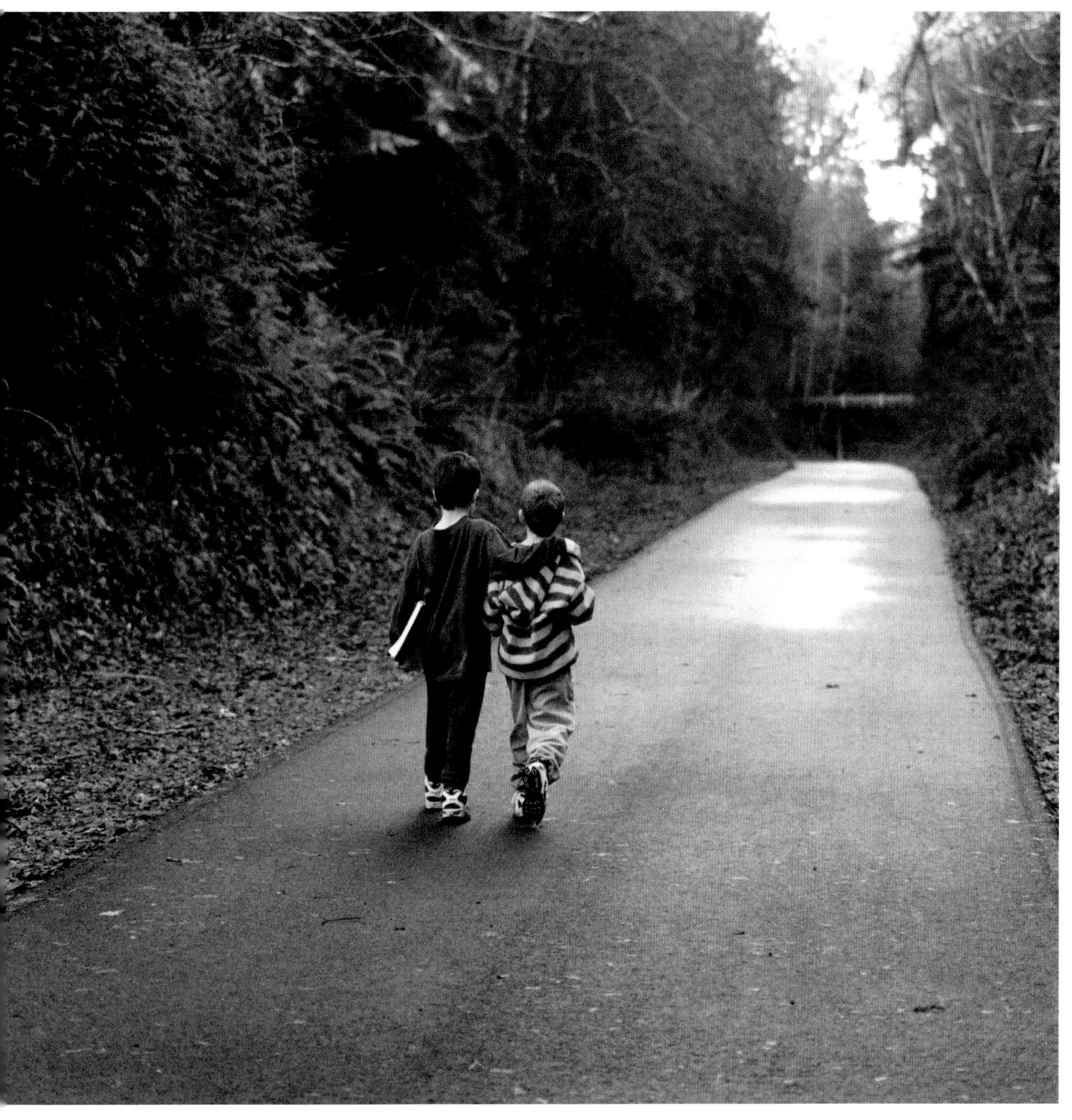

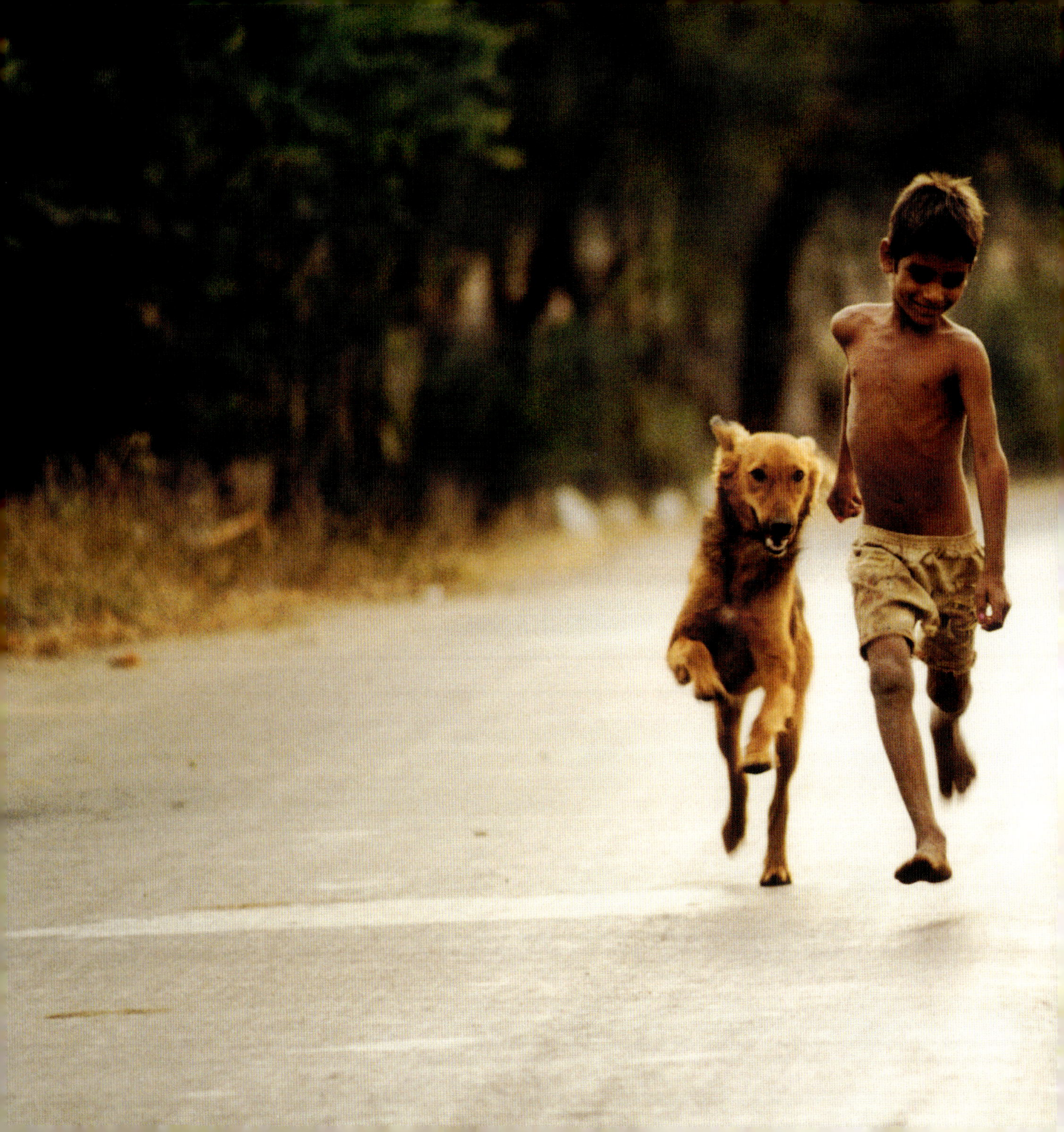

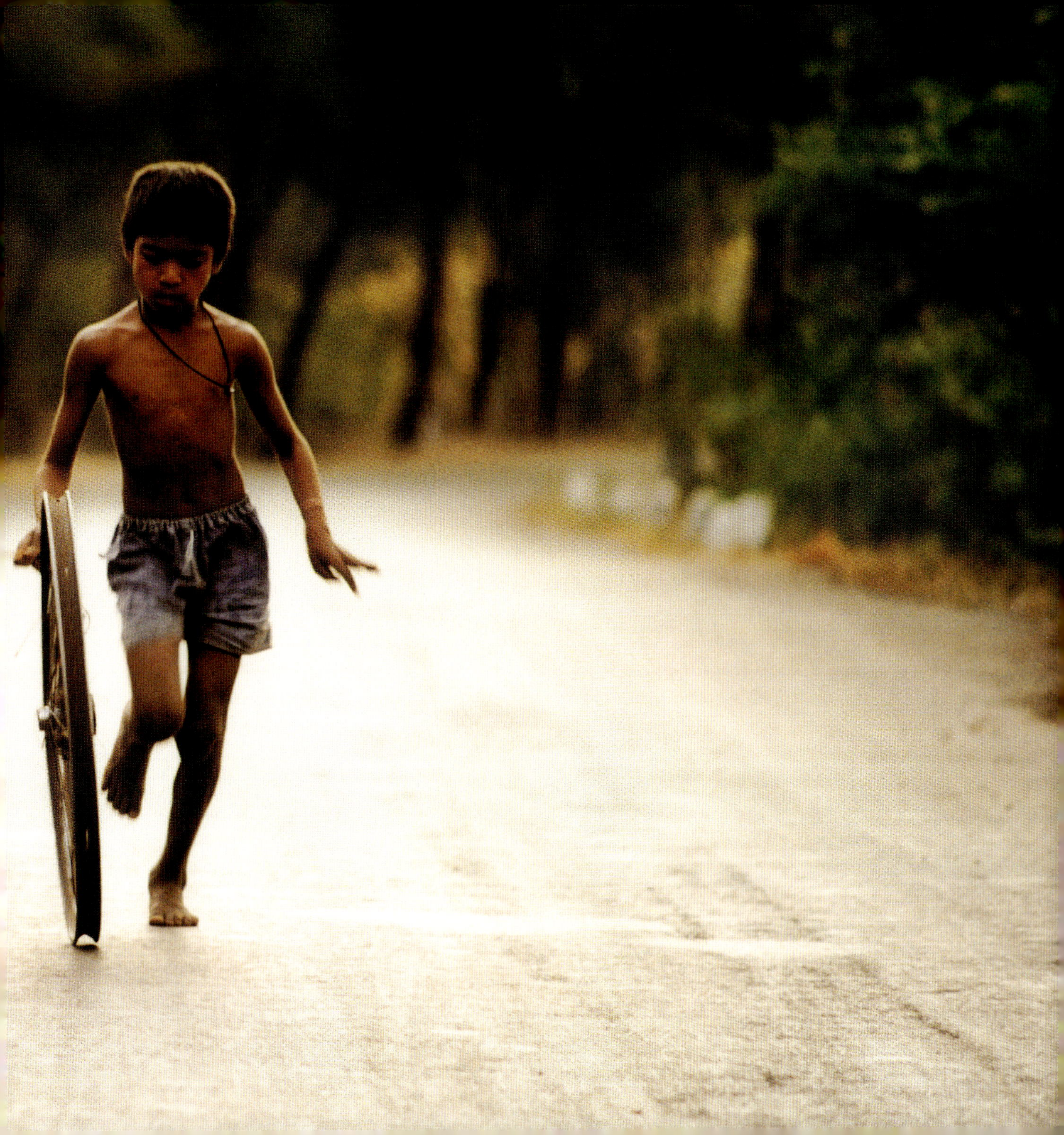

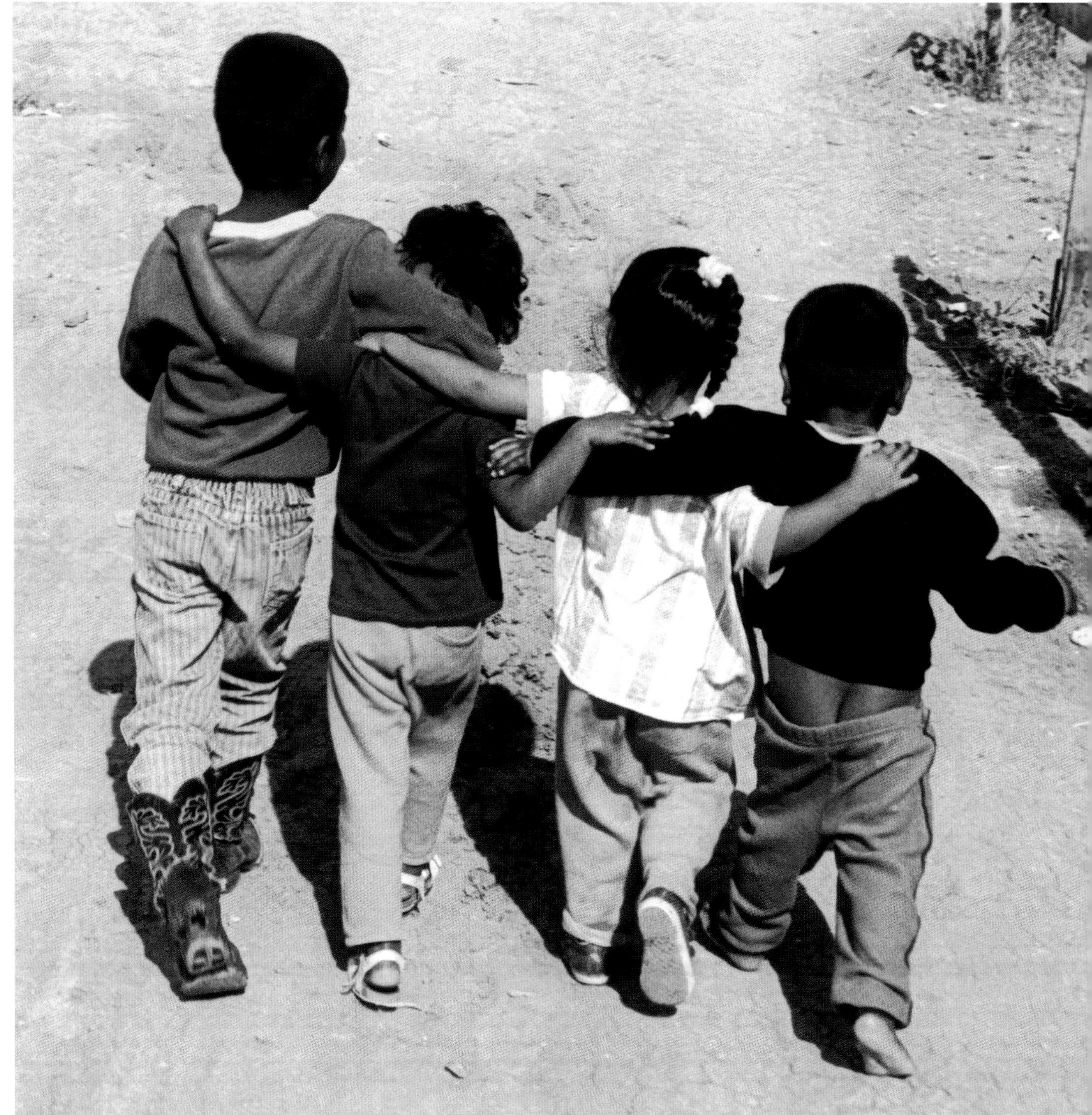

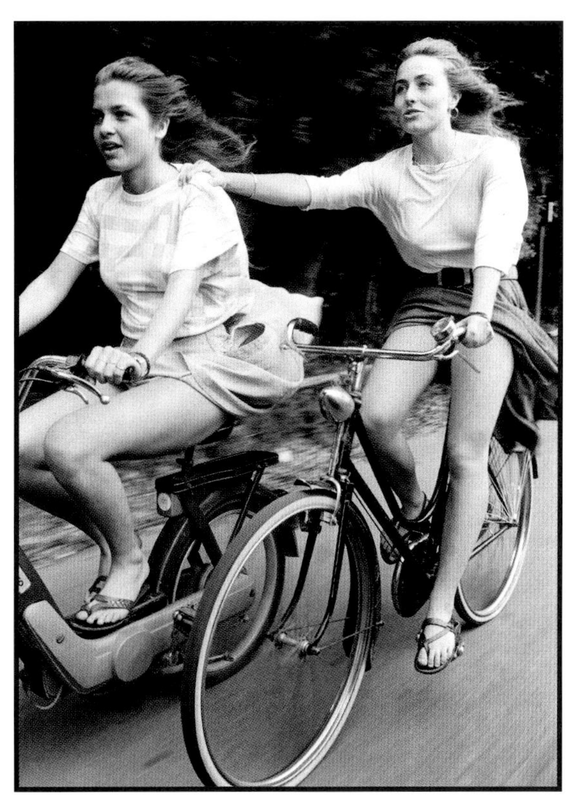

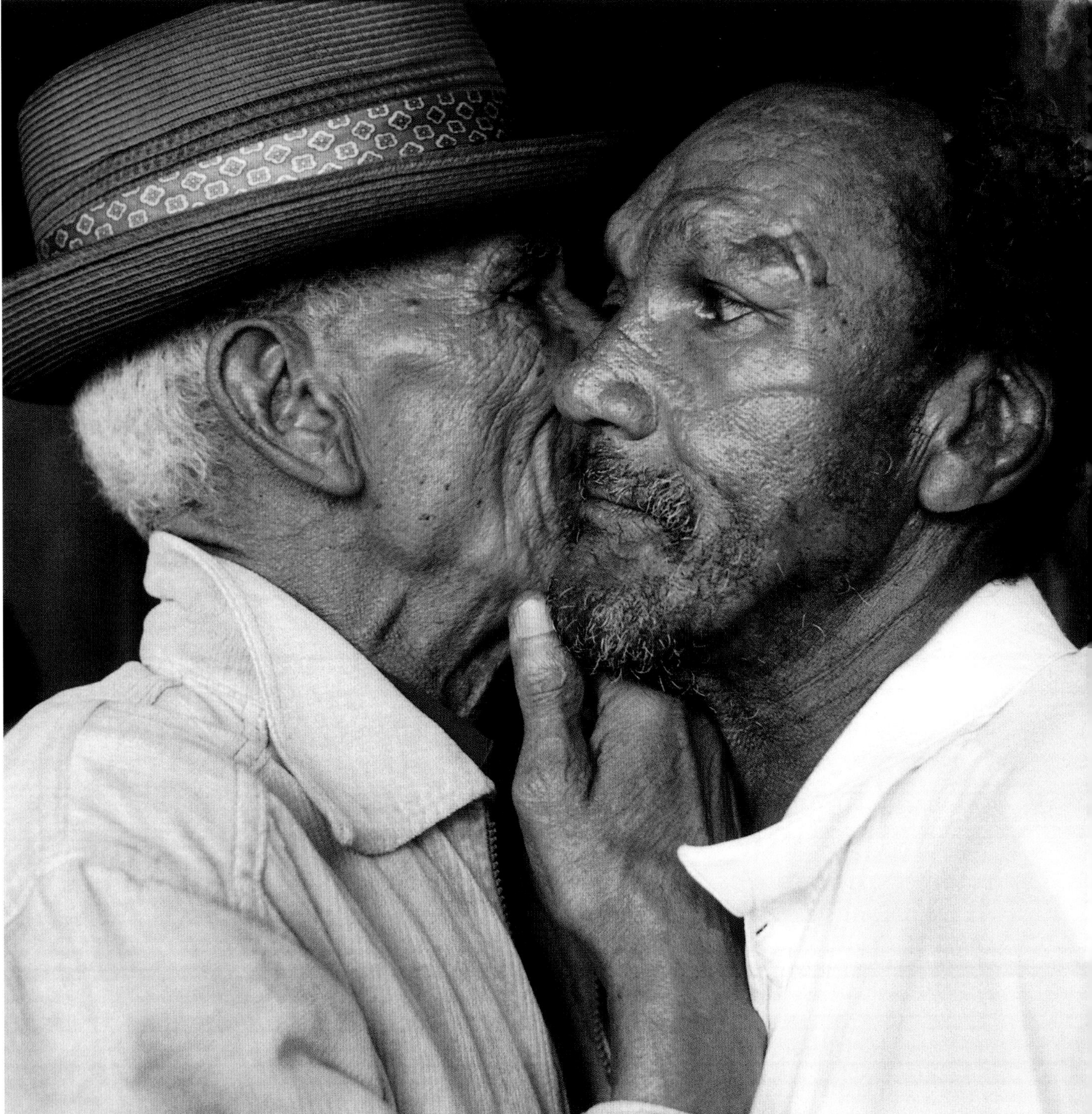

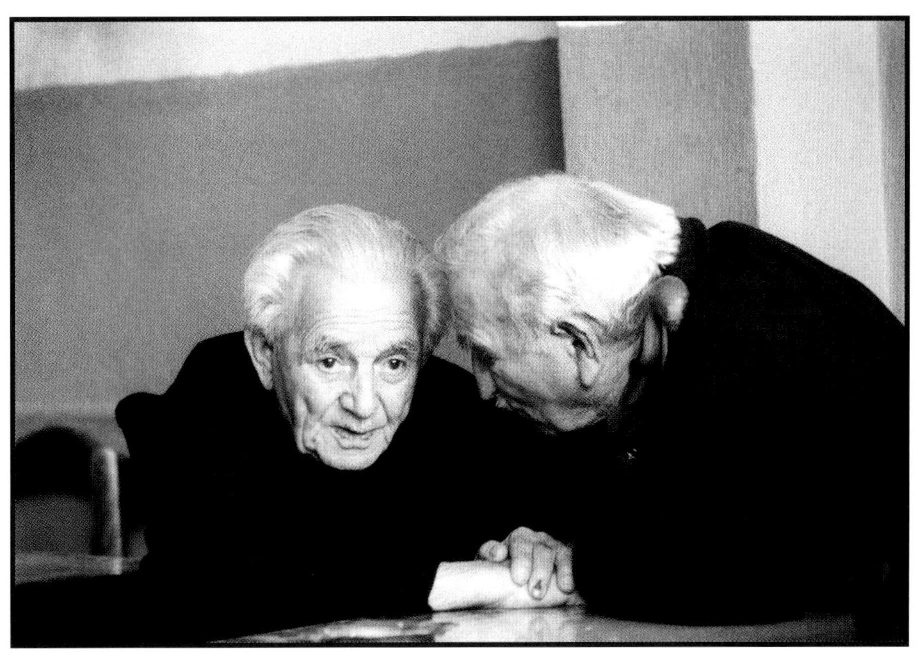

Kind words can be short and easy to speak but their echoes are truly endless.

[MOTHER TERESA]

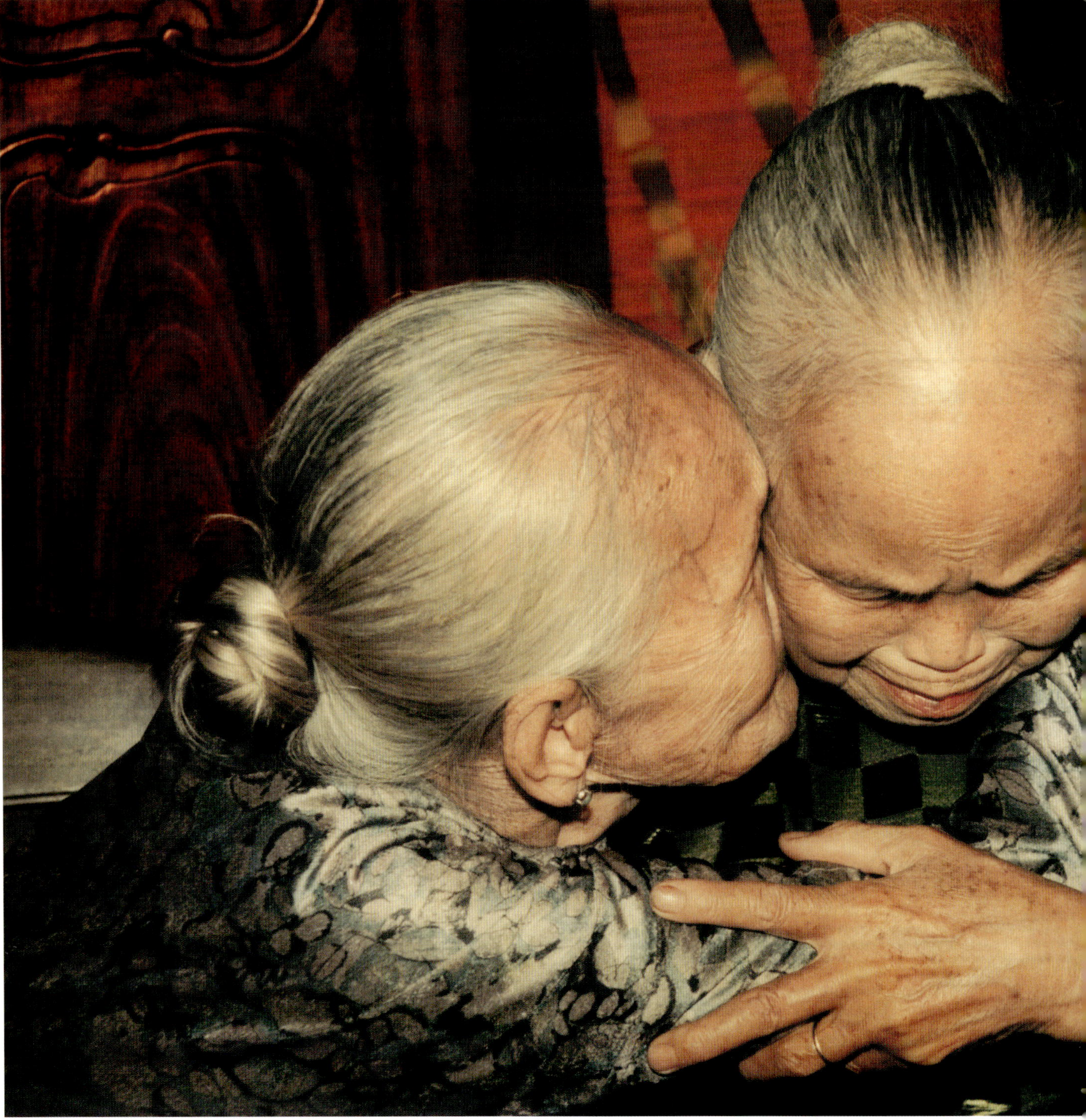

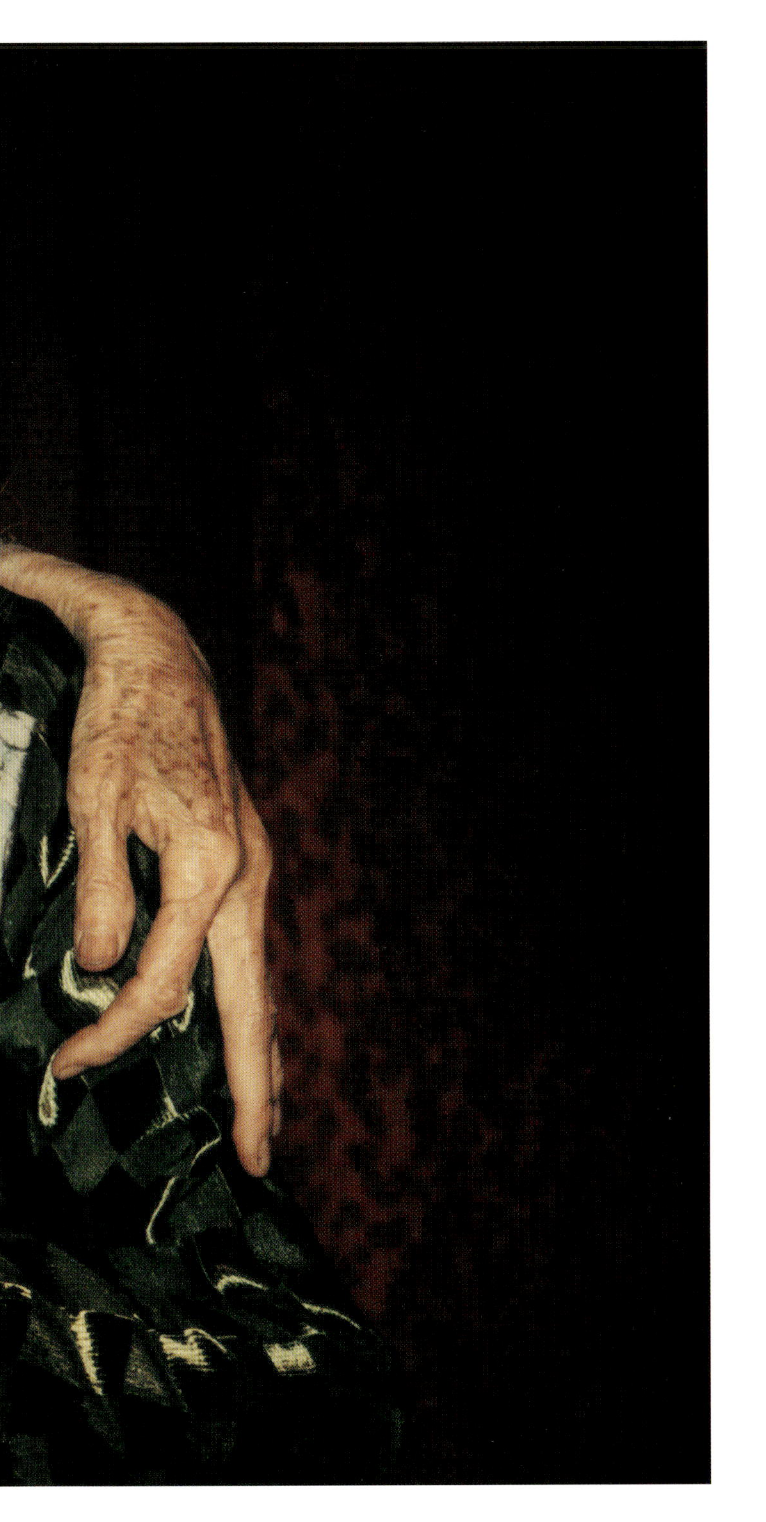

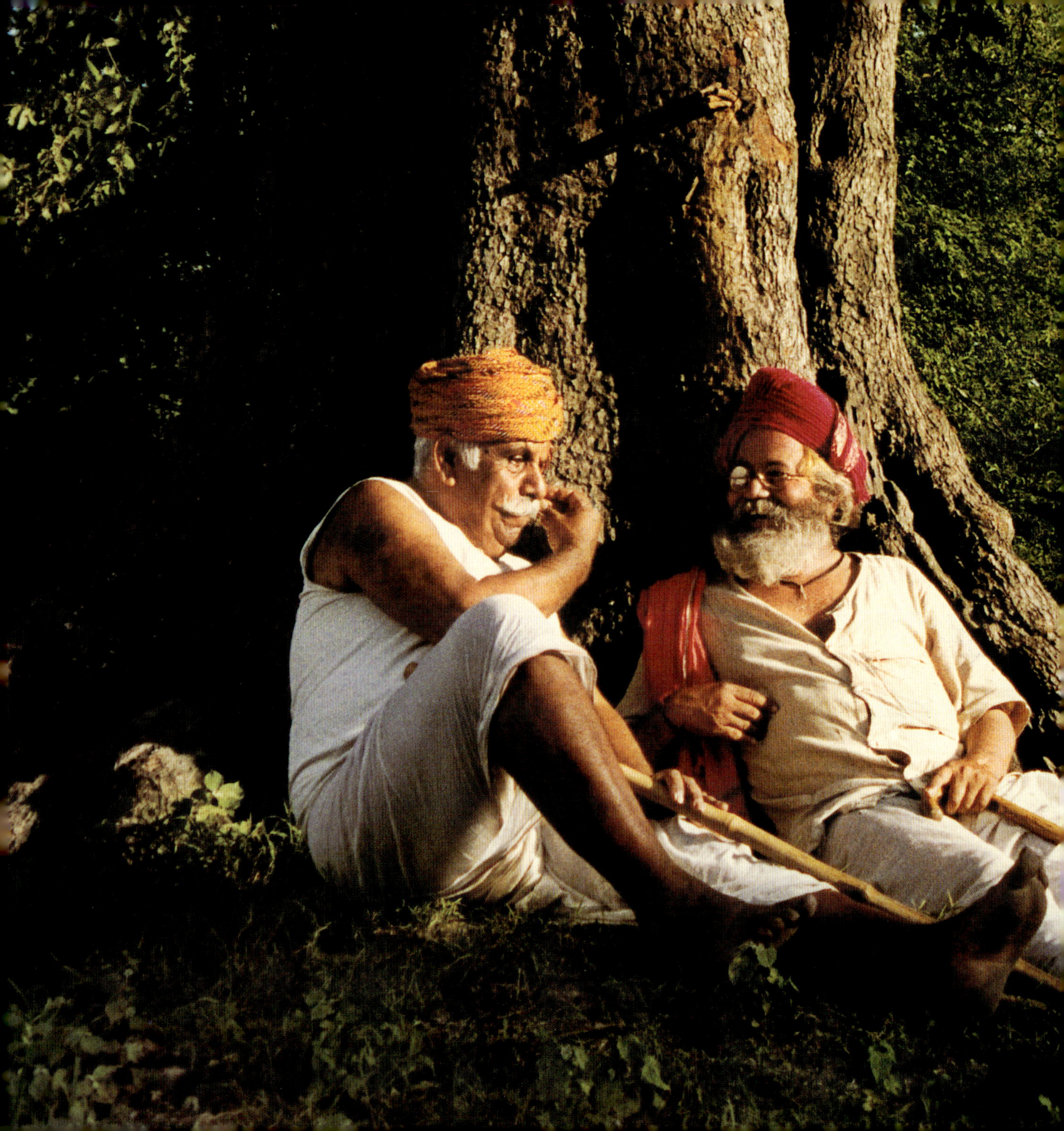

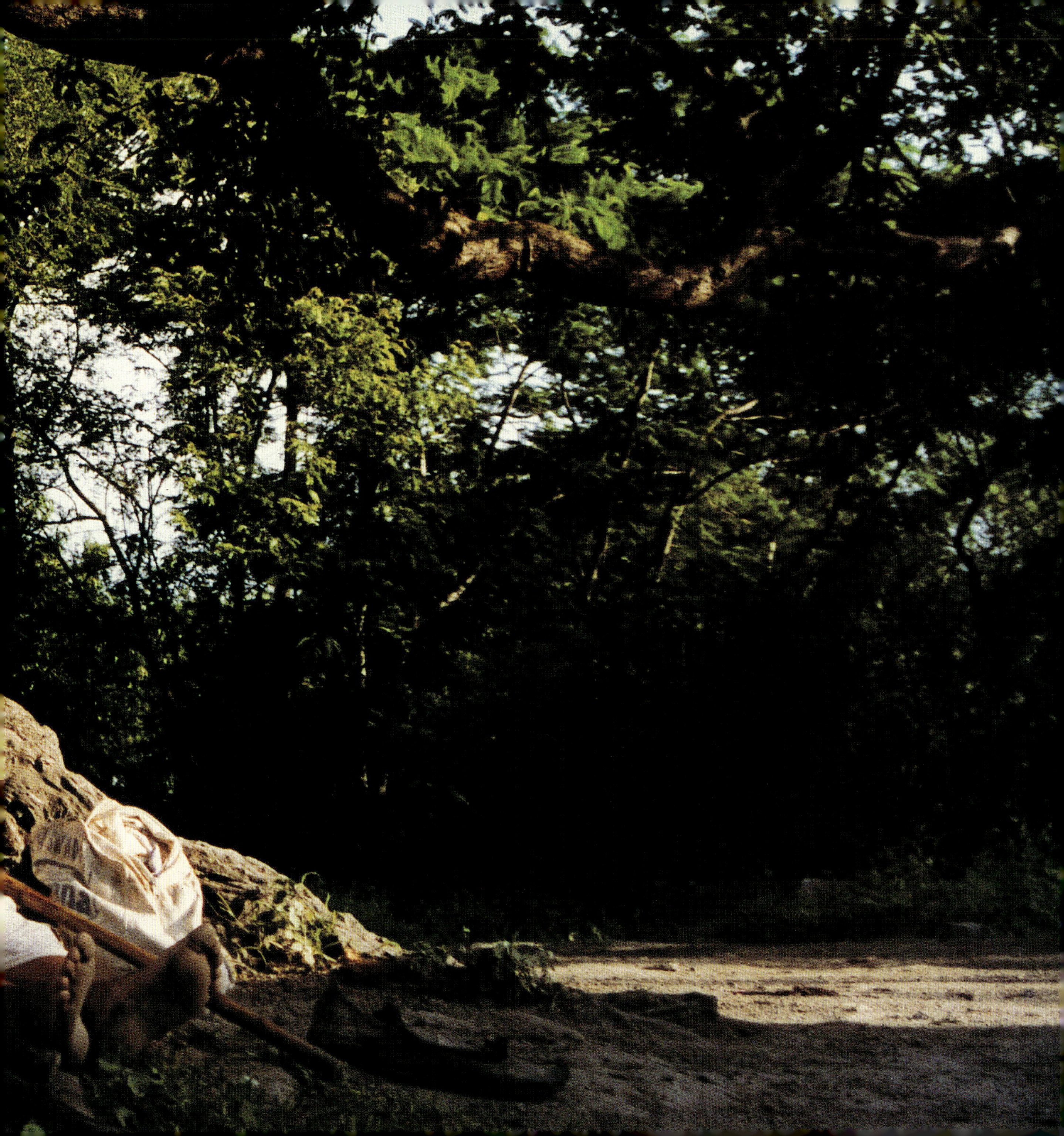

In the sweetness of friendship
let there be **laughter** and sharing of pleasures.

[KAHLIL GIBRAN]

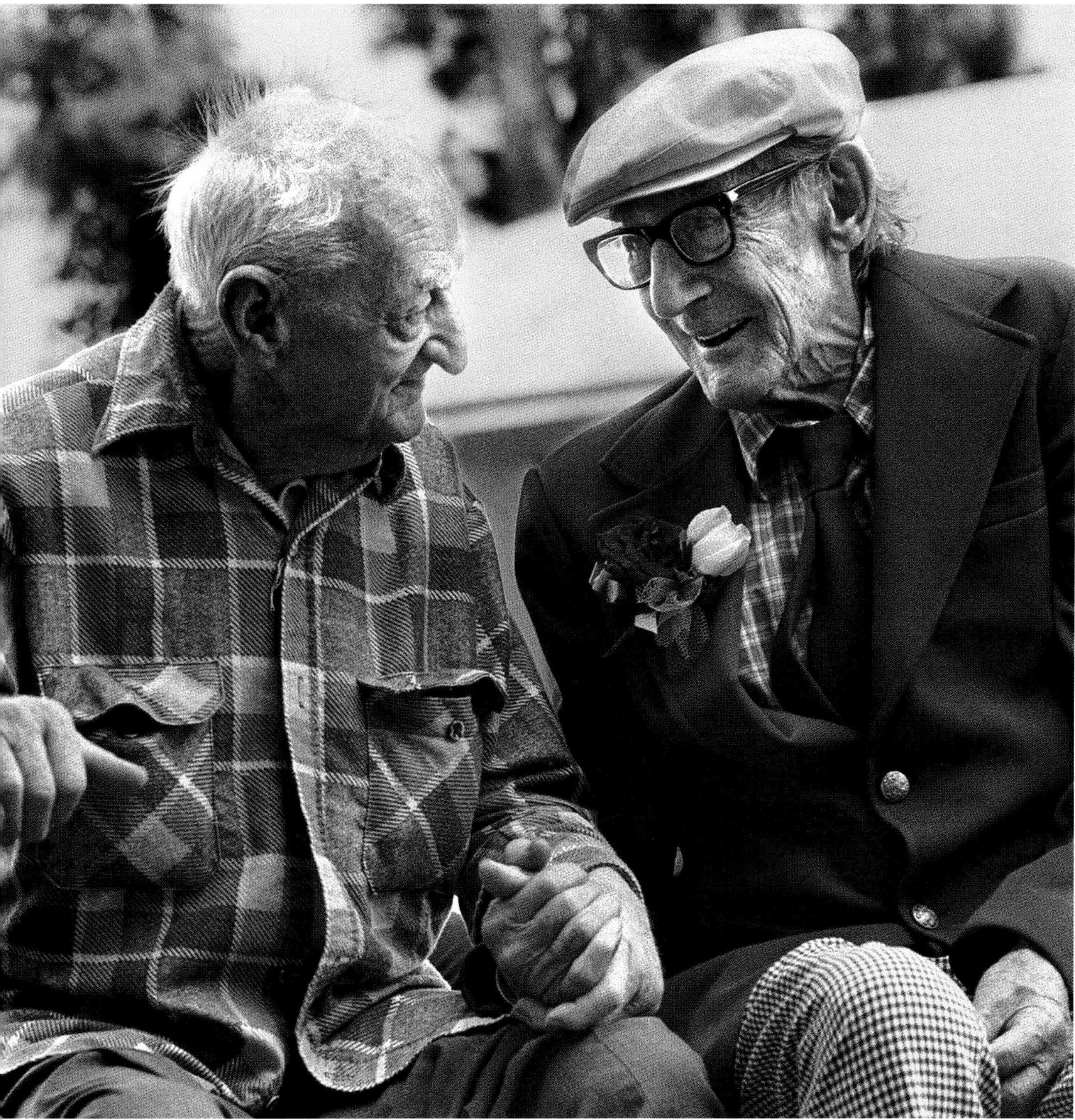

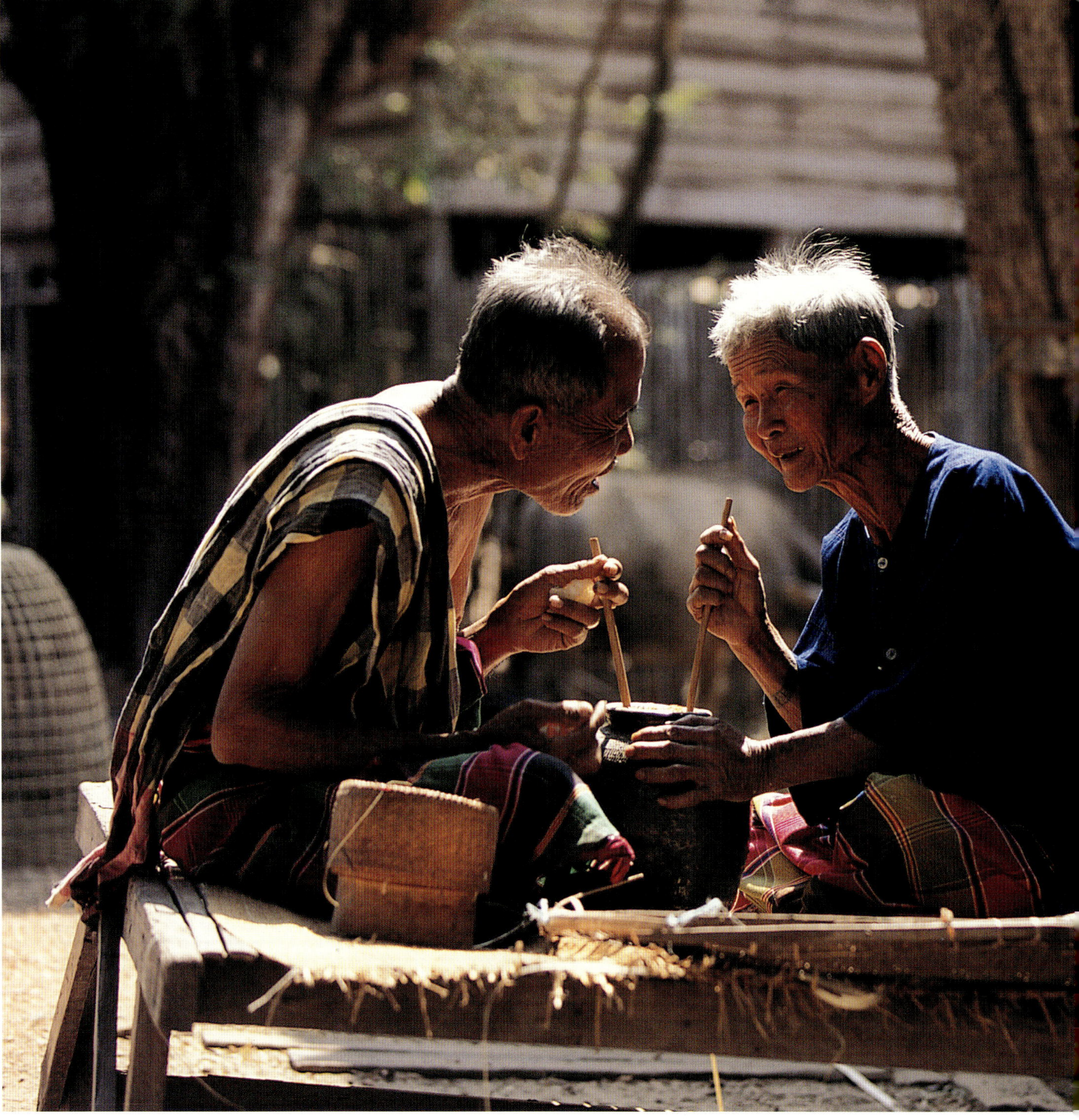

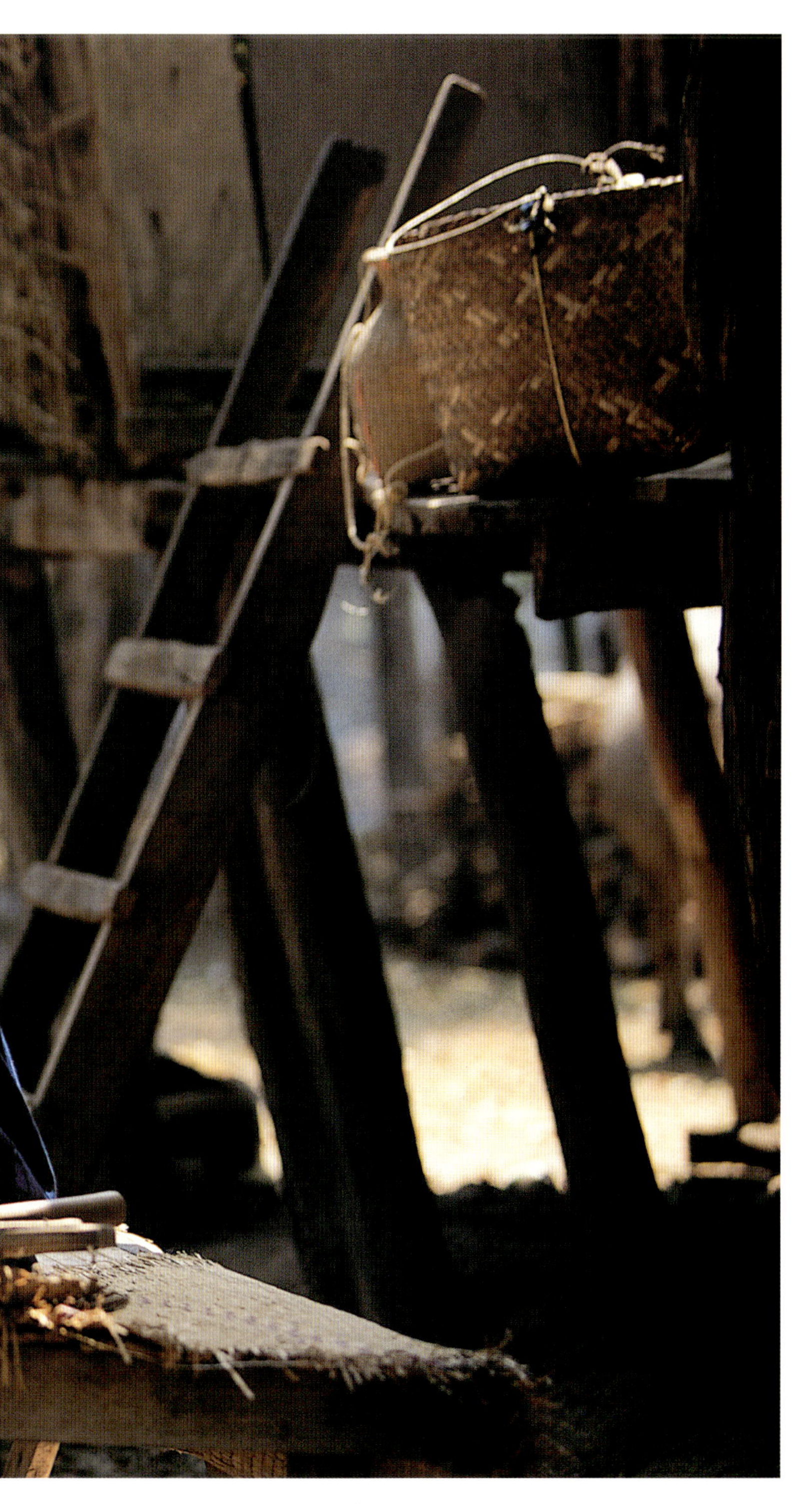

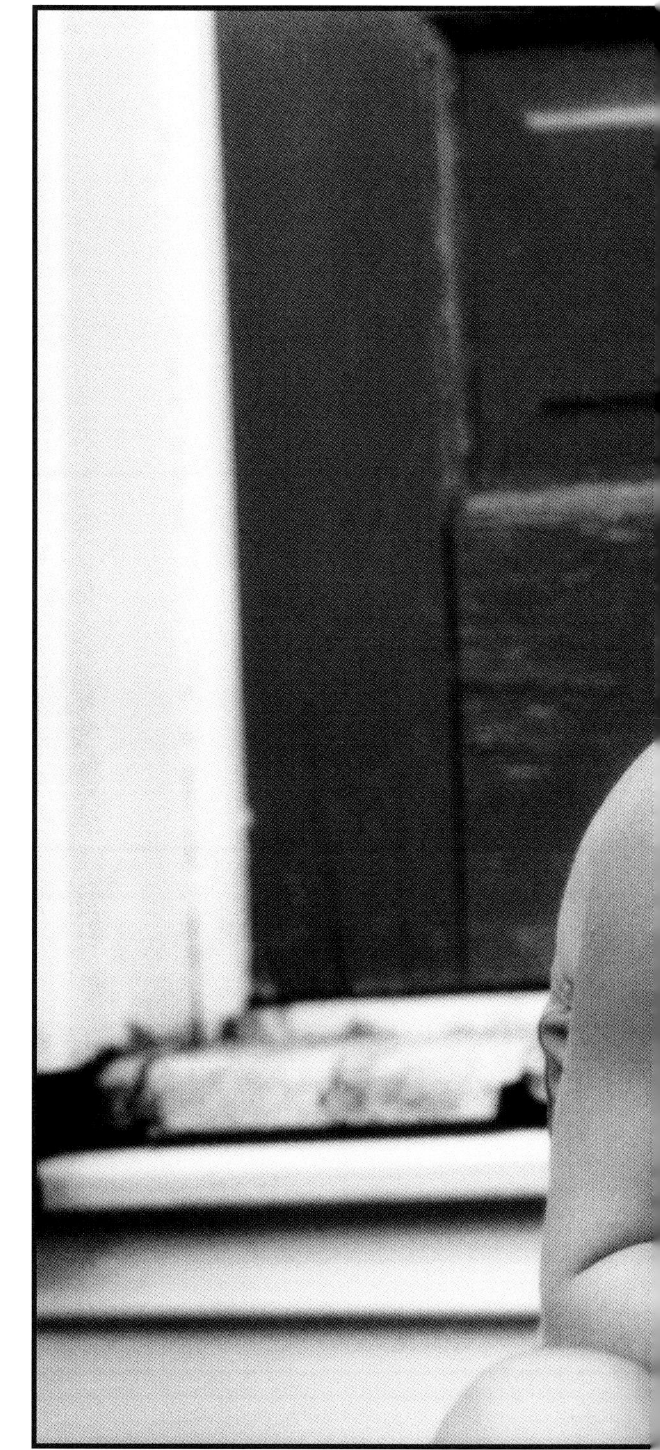

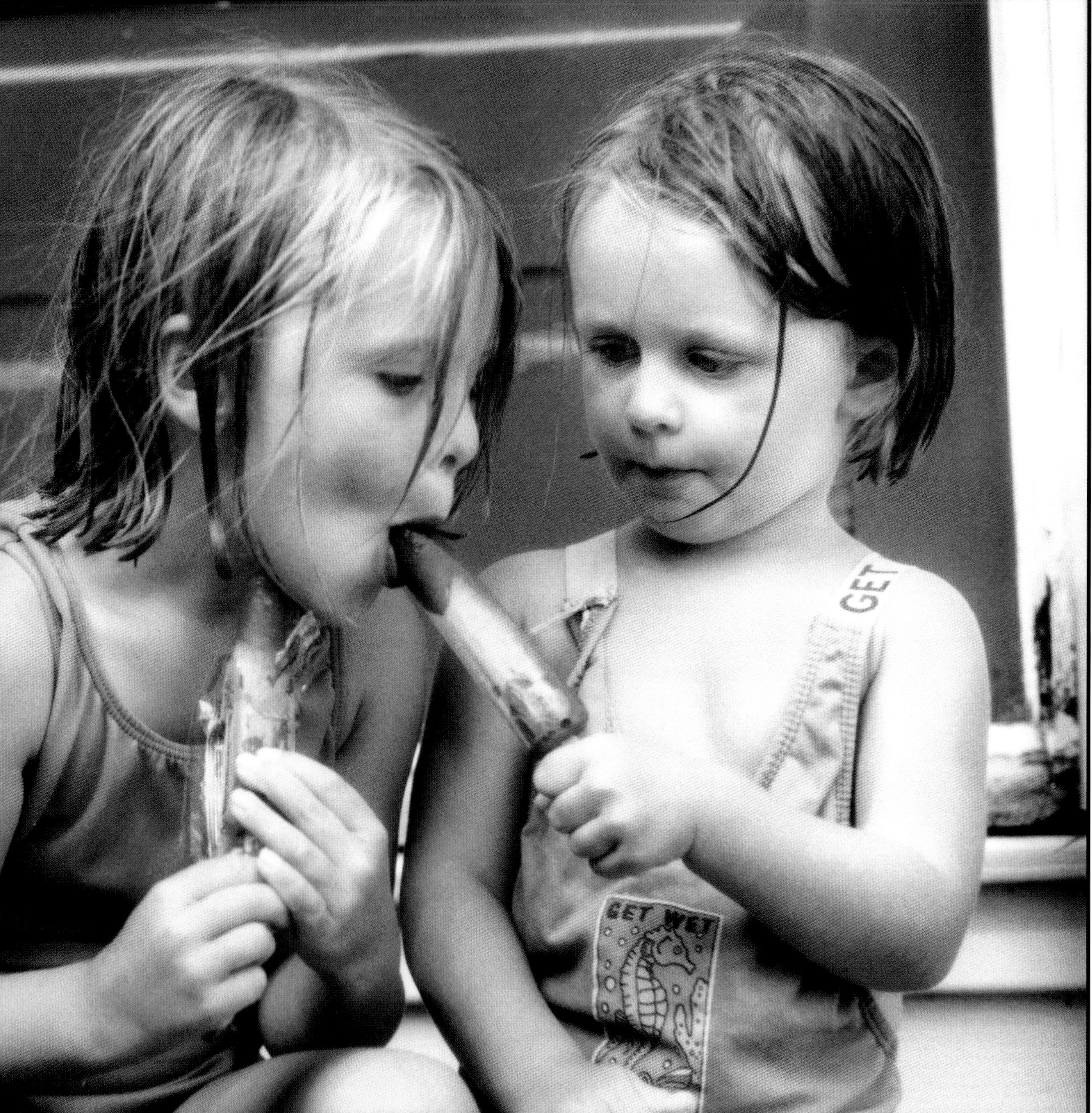
GET
GET WET

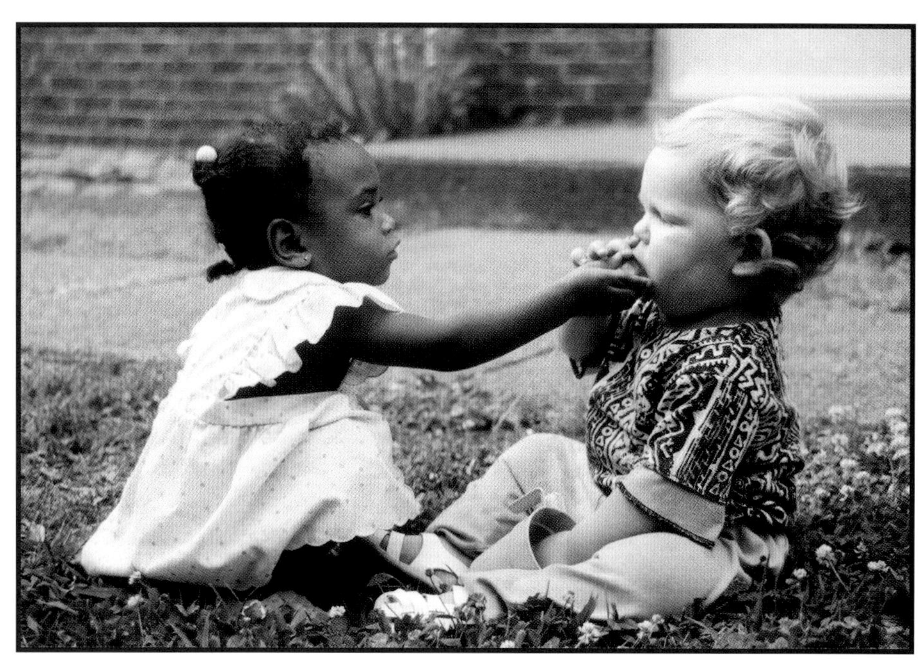

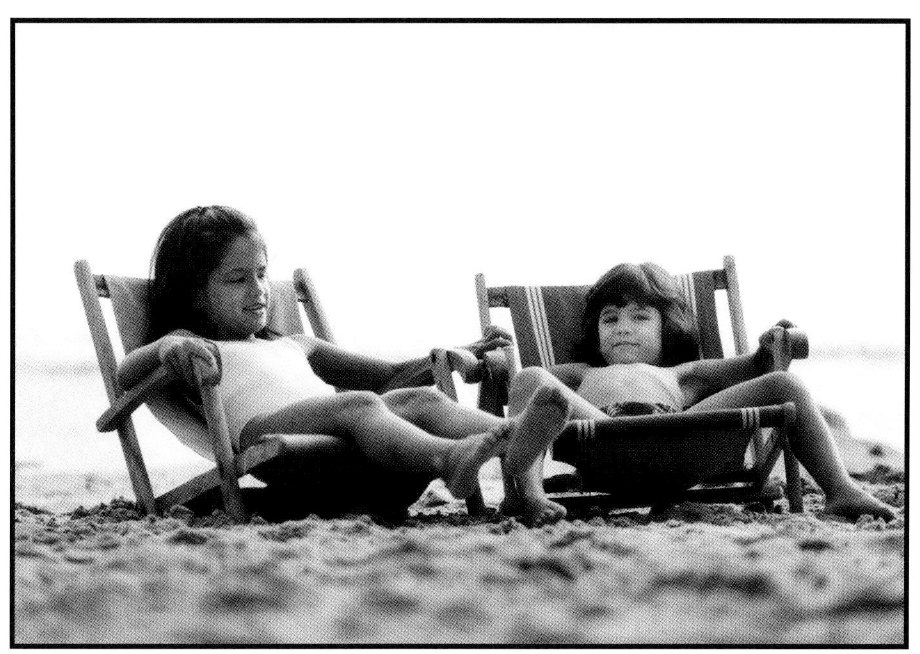

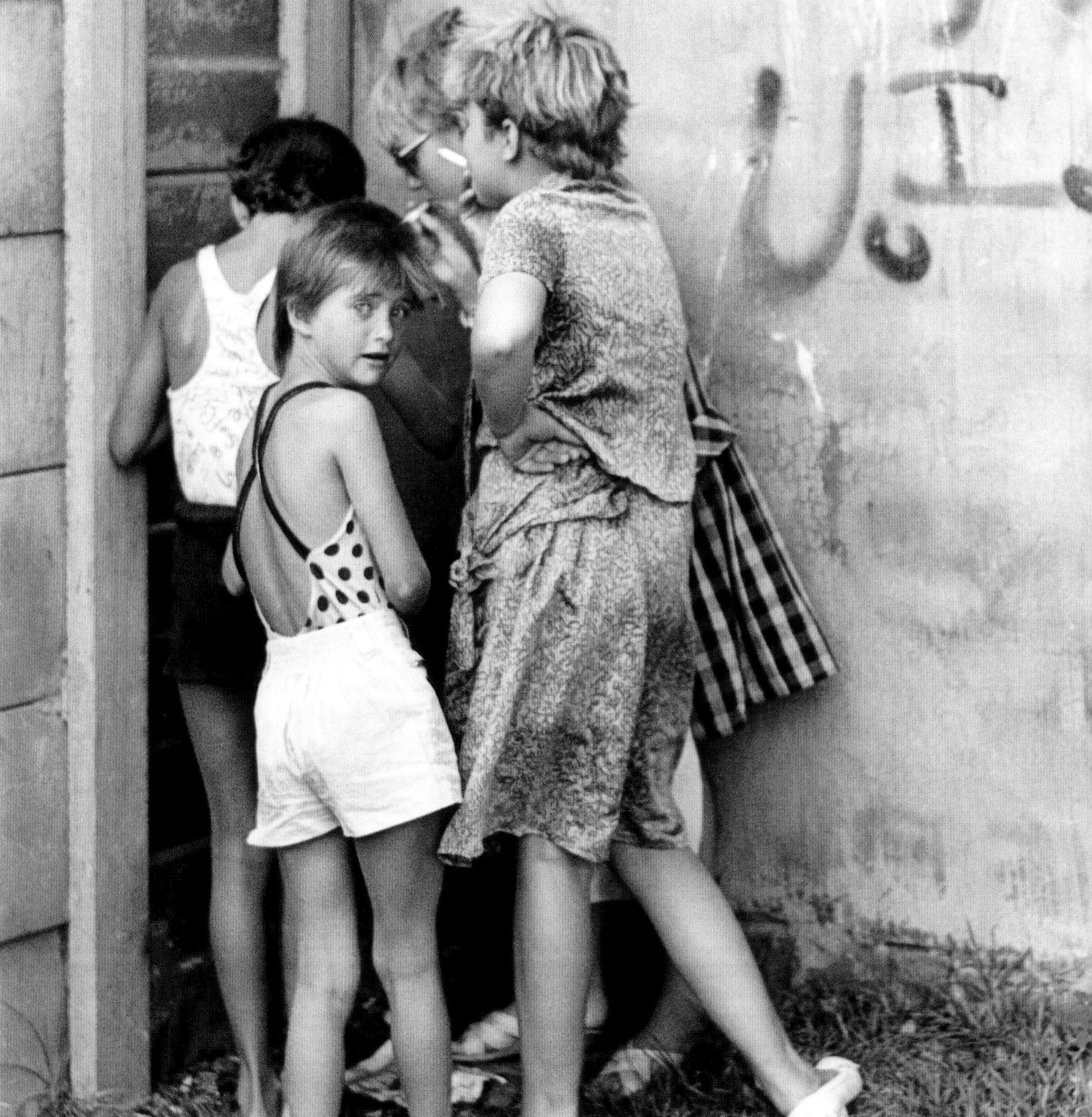

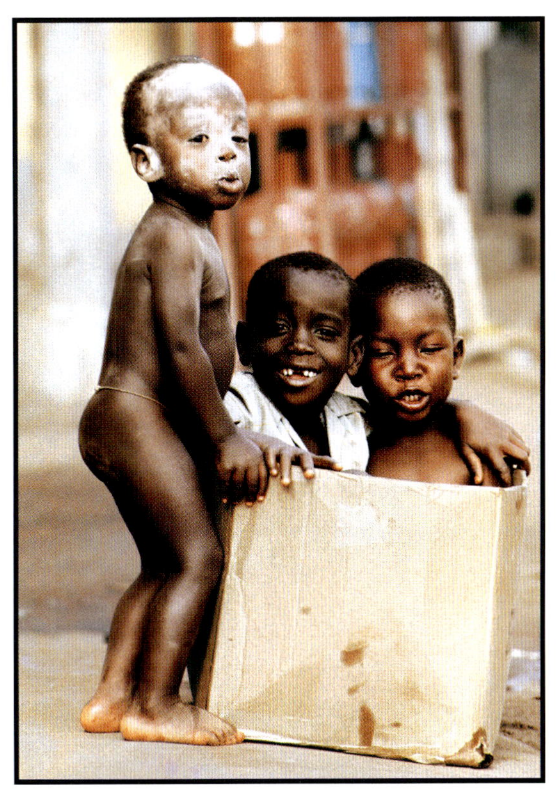

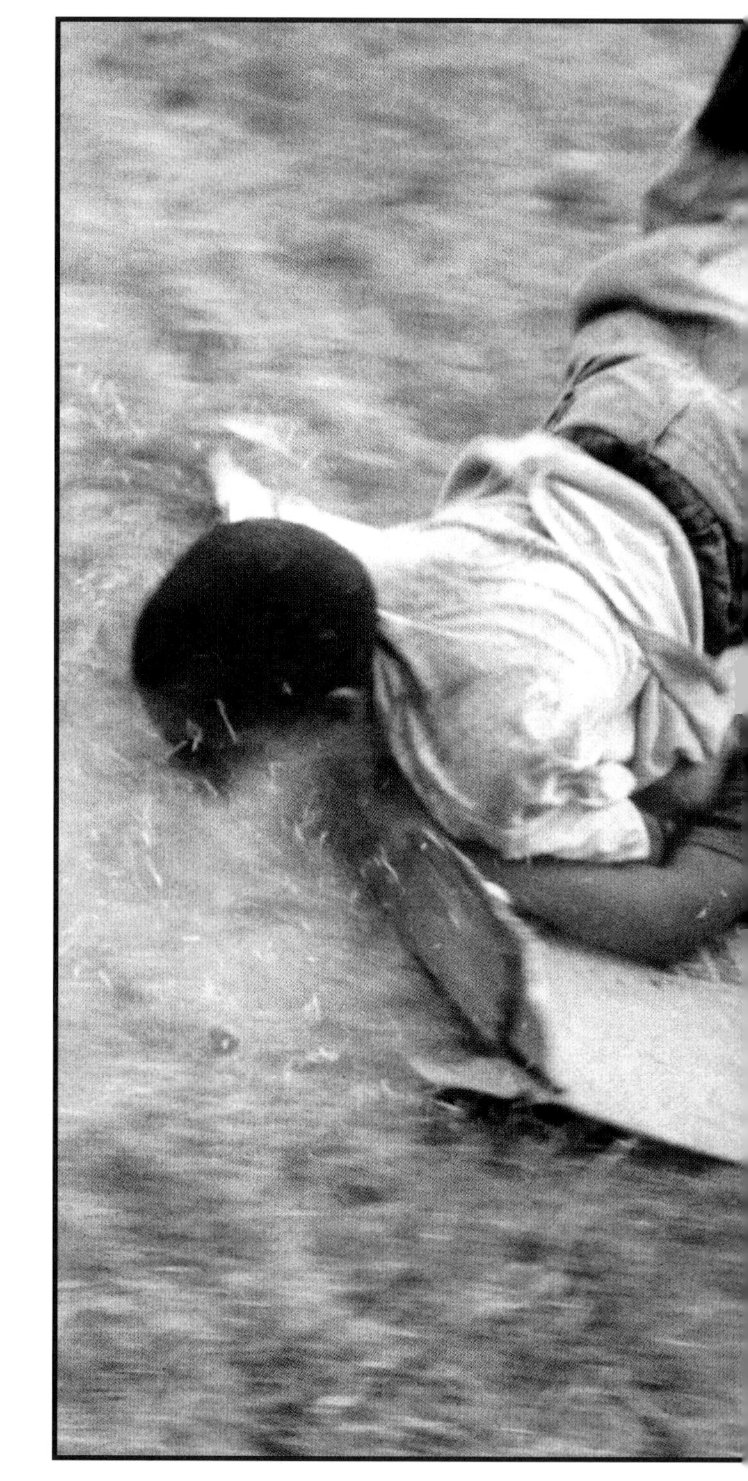

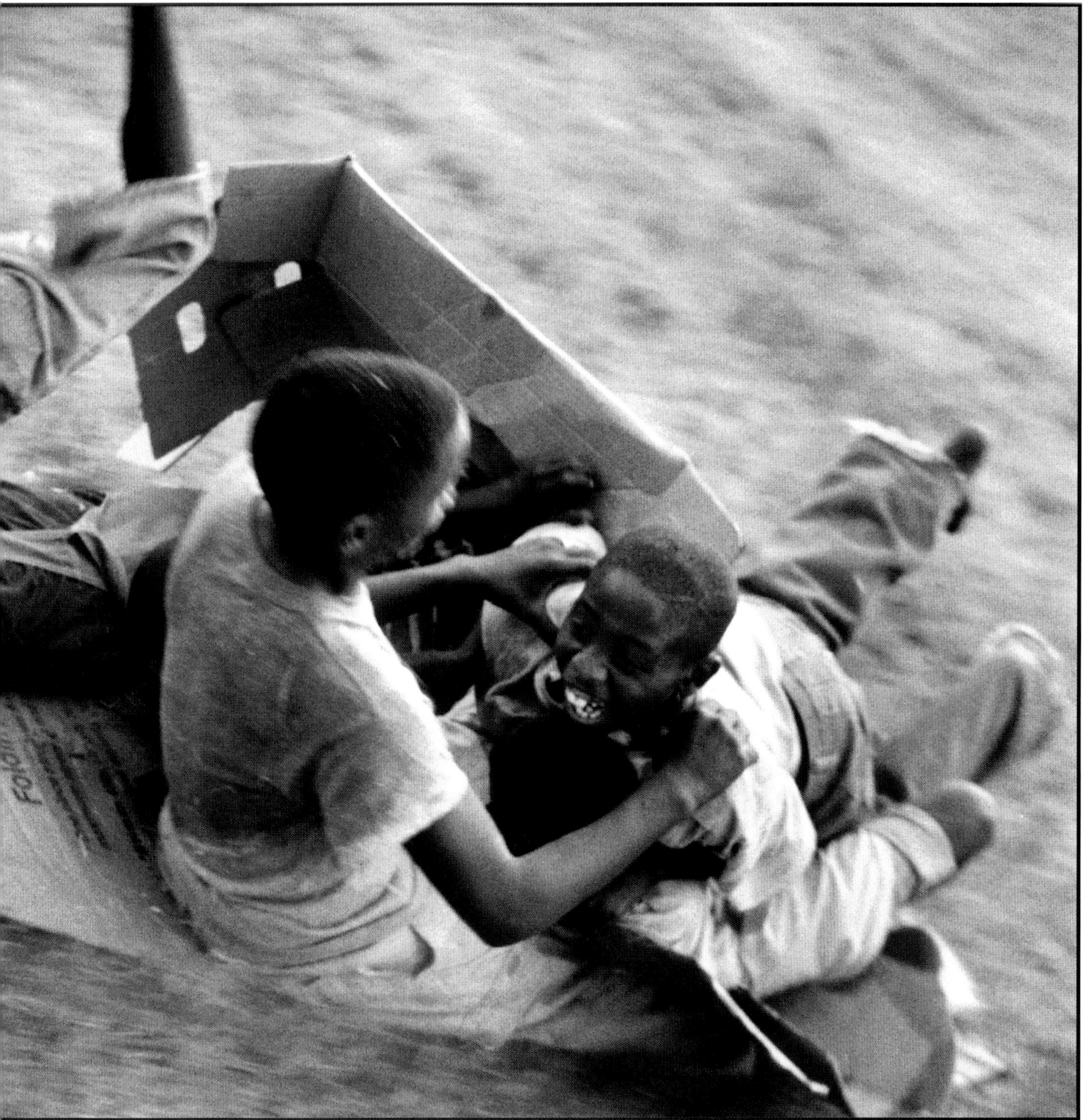

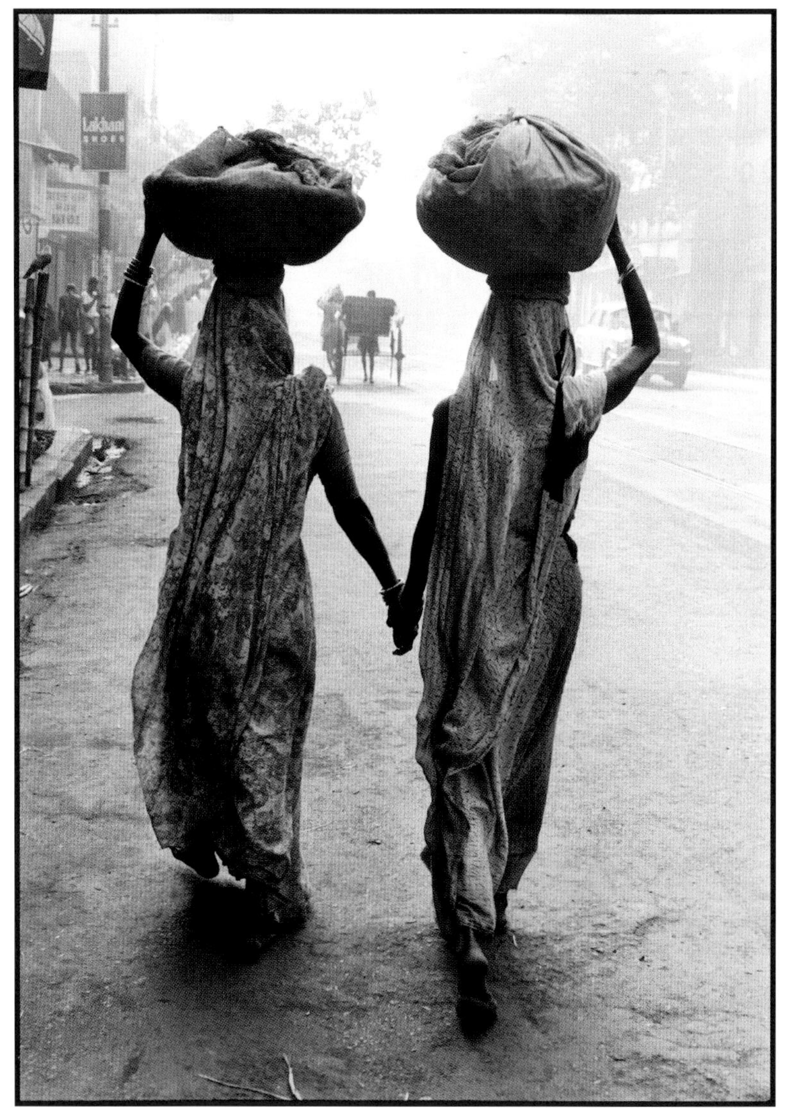

Don’t walk in front of me,
I may not follow.
Don’t walk behind me,
I may not lead.
Just walk beside me and be my friend.

[ALBERT CAMUS]

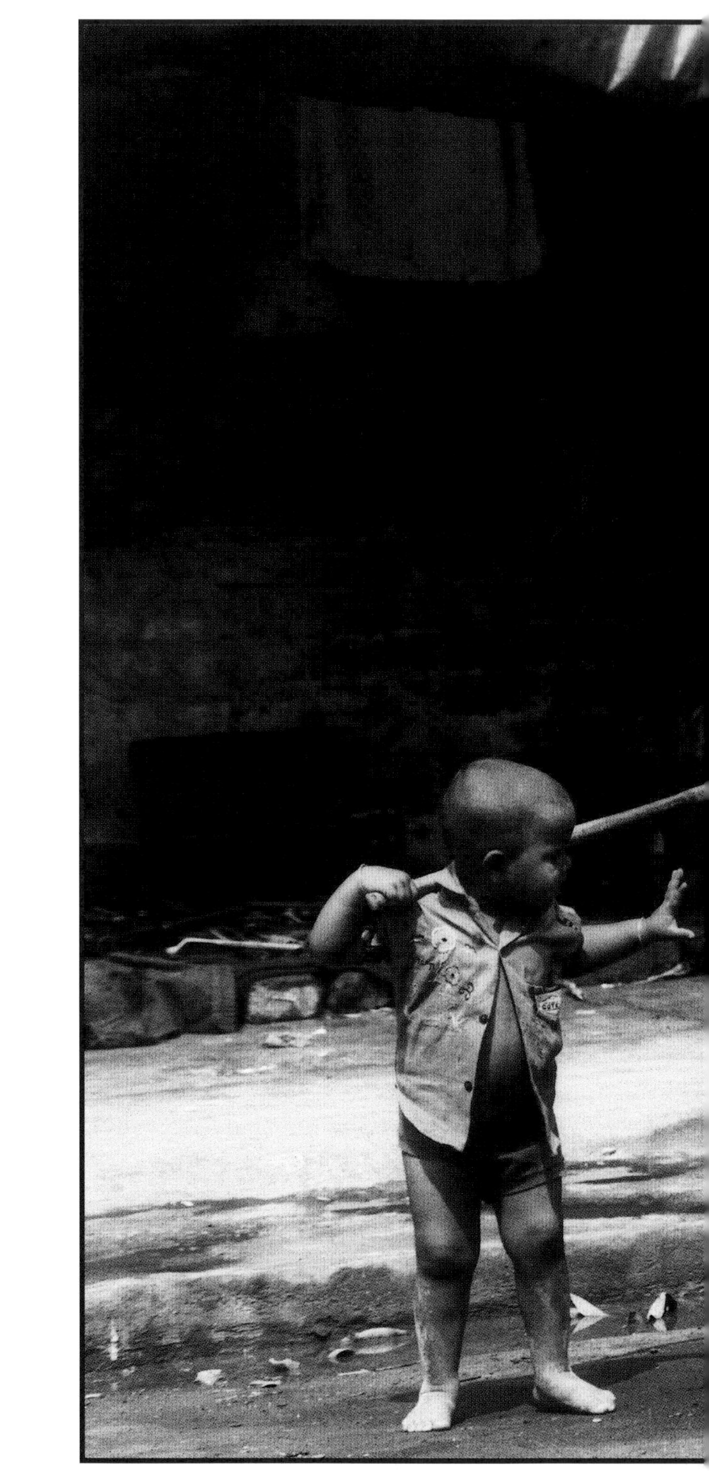

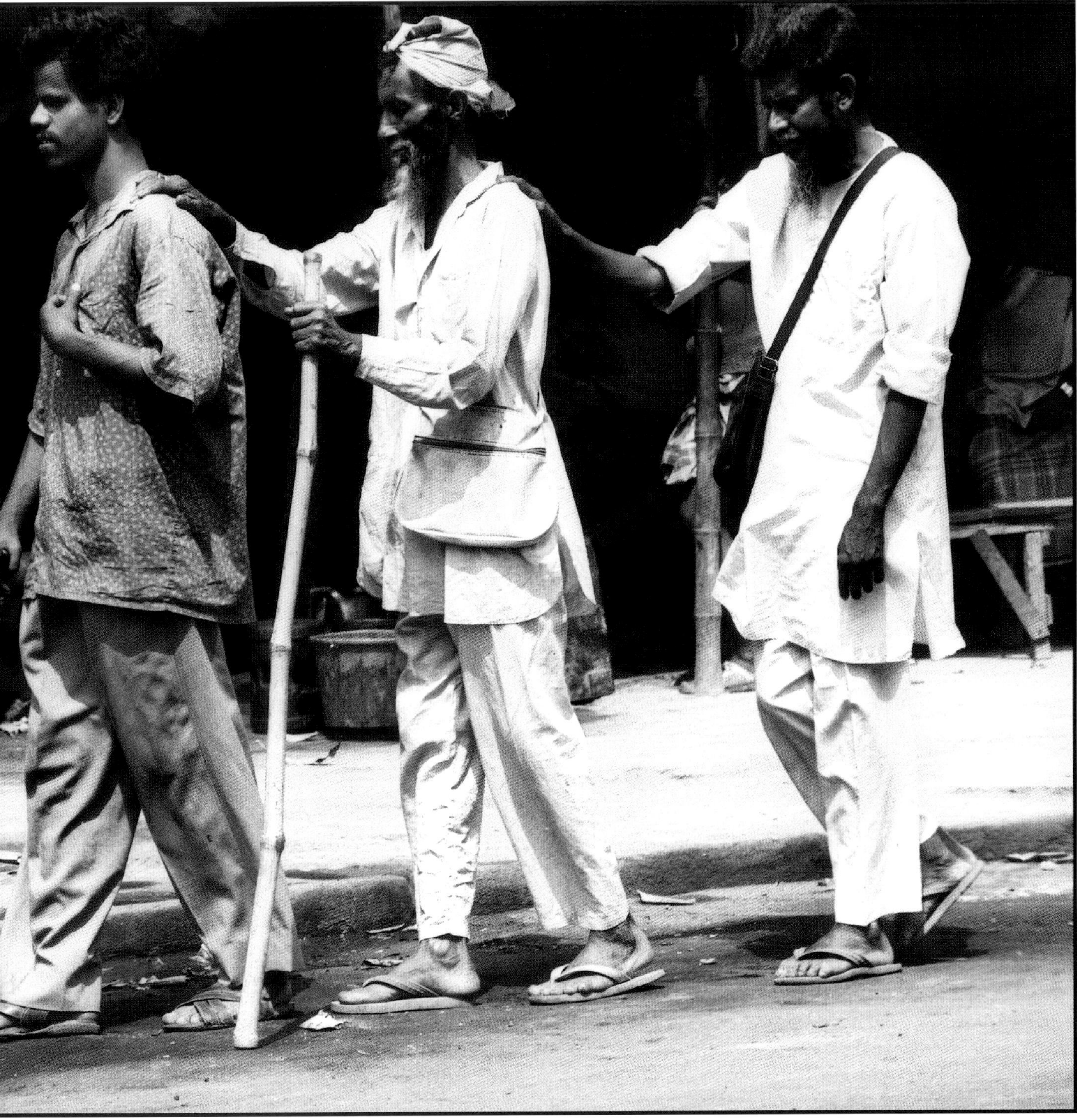

PHOTOGRAPHER CREDITS

IMAGE CAPTIONS

Cover image and pages 10–11

© Gay Block – USA
www.gayblock.com
In the bright sunshine of Miami, Florida, two friends make sure their noses are well protected as they stroll arm in arm along South Beach.

Endpaper image and page 67

© Rachel Pfotenhauer – USA
Surrounded by their family, Jean and Paul celebrate their 50th wedding anniversary at Lake Tahoe, California, USA.

page 1

© Surendra Pradhan – INDIA
Amid the paddy fields of rural India, the faces of two young workers are illuminated by laughter and friendship.

pages 2–3

© Duc Doan – VIETNAM
A fond farewell as an 88-year-old Vietnamese woman says goodbye to her childhood friend, close to death at the age of 92. This moment was captured on film in Ha Long city in the Quang Ninh province of Vietnam.

page 5

© David Williams – UK
Deckchairs on the pier provide a typical holiday setting for three friends taking a break in Brighton, in the south of England.

page 6

© Greta Pratt – USA
Summer in New Jersey, USA – best friends Axel and Colby take a break from swimming to cool off with an ice cream.

page 15

© Janice Rubin – USA
Six-year-old dancers Natasha and Mitalee look to each other for confidence before performing in front of a capacity crowd at the Houston International Festival, Texas, USA.

pages 16–17

© Dilip Padhi – INDIA
In a small village near Sambalpur, India, two young companions share a pensive moment.

pages 18–19

© Rinaldo Morelli – BRAZIL
During a visit to the zoo, young Brazilians Pietro, aged four, and Yuri, five, are inspired to create their own weird and wonderful animals.

page 20

© Davy Jones – UK
Two kilted friends stand out from the crowd at the Gay Pride Festival in London, England.

page 21

© Bernard Mendoza – USA
Elderly Ukrainian sisters caught on film during a visit to Cleveland, Ohio, USA.

pages 22–23

© Aris Munandar – INDONESIA
Amid the hustle and bustle of Wamena town in Indonesia, two Dani tribesmen find time to relax. Dressed in traditional clothing and holding home-made axes and spears, they come to Wamena to trade and socialize.

page 25

© Nicholas Ross – UK
On a dusty pavement in the slums of Bombay, India, friendship blossoms for 12-year-old Indou and her blind companion, Mala.

pages 26–27

© Serena Stevenson – NEW ZEALAND
Two elderly friends hold tightly to each other for support as they take a stroll through the cobbled streets of Göreme, a village in the Cappadocian valleys of Turkey.

page 28

© Cristina Piza – GERMANY
Musicians and old friends Ruben and Ibrahin celebrate the release of their new CD at a café in Madrid, Spain.

page 29

© Paul Knight – NEW ZEALAND
In the small, bustling town of Wajima in Japan, a local resident is eager to pass on the latest news to her friend.

page 31

© Pepe Franco – USA
In Madrid, Spain, an elderly man sings to his devoted dog while a social worker continues quietly with her chores.

page 32

© Terry Winn – NEW ZEALAND
Nine-year-old Jonathan prepares to take the plunge at his favourite swimming spot in Auckland, New Zealand. His dog Harry won't be far behind.

page 33

© Romualdas Požerskis – LITHUANIA
An enthusiastic greeting for a Lithuanian woman on the streets of the old town of Kaunas.

page 34

© Mike Ryan – USA
On the Marshall Islands in the Pacific Ocean, a young toddler stays close to her friend. Together they watch the older children dancing in an annual festival of celebration.

page 35

© Rogério Ribeiro – BRAZIL
With a box of shoe-shining equipment on his shoulder, a Brazilian boy extends a protective arm to his younger brother on the streets of Porto Alegre, in Brazil.

pages 36–37

© Jennifer Prunty – USA
Distraught at being unable to collect her social security cheque, "Mama Sue" is comforted by her companion, Dee. Both women belong to a group of homeless people, "The Family", who live together in a park in San Francisco, California, USA.

page 39

© Jon Holloway – USA
Indian children turn old tyres into new toys as they play, with the historic Taj Mahal visible in the background.

pages 40–41

© Mara Catalán – USA
High above the Annapurna Valley in Nepal, three children enjoy the simple pleasures of friendship. Perched on a precipice, the two young girls decorate their hair with freshly picked flowers.

page 42

© Alvein Damardanto – INDONESIA
After a game of soccer, two young players relive the moments of the match as they sit in the window of an old castle in Jogjakarta, Indonesia.

page 43

© Shannon Eckstein – CANADA
The rain has stopped in Chilliwack, British Columbia, Canada, and 18-month-old Kiana can't wait to explore a new puddle with the help of her puppies, Tasia and Belle.

pages 44-45

© Hank Willis Thomas – USA
Three friends compose their own picture within a picture at a Million Women March in Philadelphia, Pennsylvania, USA.

pages 46-47

© William Foley – USA
The sky's the limit for two young girls in Beirut, Lebanon. Their playground is an old sports stadium which became home to hundreds of refugees following the Israeli invasion of 1982.

page 49

© Paz Errázuriz – CHILE
Outside Santiago market in Chile, three cigarette sellers find that old crates make excellent seats when you want to catch up with friends.

pages 50-51

© Francesca Mancini – ITALY
A moment of solidarity as a young Kosovan woman embraces her friend whose husband has been killed by a mine.

page 52

© Amelia Panico – USA
In New York, a compassionate and loving moment is shared between a young nurse, Susan, and her 97-year-old patient, Carolina.

page 53

© Nathan Machain – USA
On a street in San Bernardino, California, two homeless women clasp each other in an affectionate embrace.

pages 54–55

© Faisal M D Nurul Huda – BANGLADESH
To celebrate their reunion after six years, cousins from the Marma tribe in Bangladesh smoke traditional hand-made cigars.

page 57

© Simon Lynn – NEW ZEALAND
On the shore of Lake Rotorua in New Zealand, two Maori brothers are engaged in a "hongi" – an exchange of breath as a form of greeting.

pages 58–59

© P Kevin Morley – USA
An elderly stranger reaches out to baby Jeffrey, 15 months, as they wait for a bus in Richmond, Virginia, USA.

page 60

© Viktor Kolar – CZECH REPUBLIC
Church-goers make their way carefully to mass in Karvina, Czech Republic. Their nearby church gradually sank 27 metres following long-term mining in the town.

page 61

© Gail Harvey – CANADA
On a cold day on the beach at Brighton, on England's south coast, a group of pensioners warm to each other's company.

page 62

© Marianna Cappelli – ITALY
The natural curiosity of the photographer's four-year-old daughter Martina and her friend Esther brings new discoveries on a beach in Sardinia, Italy.

page 63

© Lance Jones – USA
Friendship means playing on the same side – a young soccer team in Belfast, Northern Ireland.

pages 64-65

© Damrong Juntawonsup – THAILAND
In a rural village in the Chiangrai province of Thailand, children cheer home the winner of a running race.

page 66

© Vladimir Kryukov – RUSSIA
After a swim in the chilly waters of a Moscow river, a Russian couple steal the show with a display of affection.

page 68

© Bill Frantz – USA
Budding saxophonist Sarah, aged two, entertains her baby sister, Leslie, in Wisconsin, USA.

page 69

© Darien Mejía-Olivares – USA
As two-year-old toddlers Harry and Margaret take to the floor in New York, USA, they can't resist giving each other a hug.

pages 70–71

© Tetsuaki Oda – JAPAN
Two children are happy to amuse themselves during the interval of an outdoor music concert in Linköping, Sweden.

pages 72–73

© Yorghos Kontaxis – USA
Coney Island in New York, USA – six friends turn a sandy beach into a dance floor to the delight of their enthusiastic audience.

page 75

© Jana Noseková – CZECH REPUBLIC
Fun and games in the water for a group of bathers in Constanze, Romania.

© Simon Roberts – UK
These men belong to a nudist group who meet to play games and enjoy the sunshine and freedom of the Arizona desert.

pages 76–77

© Peter Gabriel – USA

A fashion-conscious trio discover the perfect accessory as they sit in a café in New York.

pages 78

© Robin Sparks Daugherty – USA

During a summer drought in New Mexico, USA, three friends prove that there is still fun to be had with only two inches of water in the pool.

pages 79

© Ted Polumbaum – USA

Members of the "Polar Bear Club" aren't worried by the cold temperatures as they soak up the winter sun on Coney Island, New York. The onlookers don't share the same dress code.

pages 80–81

© Seifollah Samadian Ahangar – IRAN

Friends Asadollah and Mohammad strike the traditional and historic pose of Iranian athletes for this photograph in Orumieh, Iran.

pages 82–83

© Bernard Poh Lye Kiat – SINGAPORE

As the photographer gets his shop window ready for the festive season, his cheeky young relatives do their best to distract him.

page 85

© Joan Sullivan – CANADA

In the foothills of the Himalayas, a Nepalese grandfather looks after his two grandchildren while he catches up on news brought from Kathmandu by a young porter.

page 86

© Dô˜ Anh Tuấn – VIETNAM

Smiles light up the faces of three old friends when they are reunited at a festival in Bac Ninh town, Vietnam.

page 87

© David Tak-Wai Leung – CANADA

Two Mayan children share laughter and cuddles in Panajachel, Guatemala.

pages 88–89

© Malie Rich-Griffith – USA

Laughter is infectious for three friends from Mgahinga village, Uganda.

page 90

© Kostas Argyris – GREECE

A Greek lunch companion can't disguise a yawn after a fishy repast in Thessaloniki.

page 91

© Doreen Hemp – SOUTH AFRICA

Dressed in the traditional beaded loincloths and necklaces of their tribe, two Ndebele children play outside their home in Kwandebele, South Africa.

pages 92–93

© Marianne Thomas – USA

John David Bethel gives Eric Hinze, his "little buddy", an affectionate pat. The boys are both sufferers of spina bifida, a disease of the spinal cord. They play together while their parents attend a support group meeting in Florida, USA.

page 95

© Pat Justis – USA

A country lane in Olympia, Washington, USA, becomes an adventurous path for childhood friends Keegan, aged six, and Graeme, seven.

pages 96–97

© Dharmesh Bhavsar – CANADA

A rolling wheel leads an energetic race for three companions on a deserted road in Baroda, India.

page 98

© Michael Chiabaudo – USA

As his friends stride out along a dusty village street near Tijuana, Mexico, a young boy – and his trousers – try to keep up.

page 99

© Romano Cagnoni – ITALY

High spirits on the road to Pietrasanta, Italy, as two teenage friends ride to the beach.

page 100

© Charley Van Dugteren – SOUTH AFRICA

Two companions get close to make themselves heard in a noisy shebeen – a local pub – in Cape Town, South Africa.

page 101

© Gundula Aris Pavlos – GREECE

Old friends Blionas, 92, and Tsigaras, 90, are absorbed in each other's conversation as they sit in their overcoats in a chilly café in Grevena, Greece.

pages 102–103

© Minh Qúy – VIETNAM

An affectionate embrace as two sisters, both over the age of 80, share a private moment in Binh Duöng province, Vietnam.

pages 104–105

© Kailash Soni – INDIA

Conversation comes easily to two old friends as they relax opposite the Shiv Temple of Bilawali in Dewas, India.

page 107

© Marianne Thomas – USA

William Bossidy listens attentively to his friend John Noonan, a fellow resident at their nursing home in Florida, USA.

pages 108–109

© Sombut Ketkeaw – THAILAND

Uncle Yoo, 67, and Uncle Song, 72, unwind over a pot of "uh" – a traditional alcoholic drink – after a long day's work in the countryside of Nakornpanom, Thailand.

pages 110–111

© Linda Heim – USA

Taste testing in Averill Park, in New York state, USA – five-year-old Abigail is curious to see whether Samantha's lollipop has a different flavour from her own.

page 112

© Linda Heim – USA
Precious and Alex, find that sharing ice cubes is the perfect way to keep cool on a hot summer day in Nashville, Tennessee, USA.

page 113

© Thierry Des Ouches – FRANCE
Young sun worshippers Diane and Audrey take it easy on the beach in Noirmoutier, France. Their photographer father captures the scene.

page 114

© Antony Soicher – SOUTH AFRICA
Caught in the act – young smokers meet in the corner of a park in Johannesburg, South Africa, to enjoy a secret cigarette.

page 115

© Claude Coirault – TAHITI
A young boy – his face smeared with local medicine – soon forgets his illness when his friends arrive with their new toy, a cardboard box. This scene was captured on film in Abidjan in the Ivory Coast region of Africa.

pages 116–117

© Mark Edward Harris – USA
A cardboard box provides thrills and spills for a group of friends on a hillside in Memphis, Tennessee, USA.

page 118

© Thomas Patrick Kiernan – IRELAND
Graceful under a heavy load – two Indian women walk side by side as they carry vegetables to market in Calcutta, India.

pages 120–121

© Aranya Sen – INDIA
Six-year-old street urchin Babloo holds up his tiny hand to stop an oncoming car as he helps three blind friends to cross the road to their school in Calcutta, India.

page 128

© John A Hryniuk – CANADA
A retired Canadian war veteran shares a pensive moment with a close companion, near Ottawa, Ontario, Canada. Home is an old school bus which he shares with 15 energetic dogs.

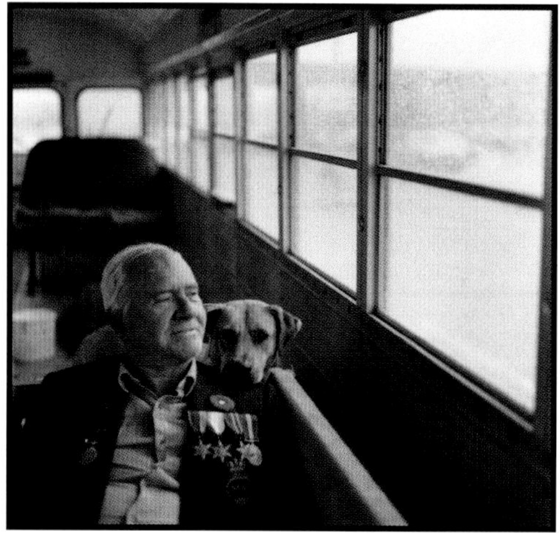

First Australian edition published in 2003 by Hodder Headline Australia Pty Limited [a member of the Hodder Headline Group],
Level 22, 201 Kent Street, Sydney NSW 2000.

First New Zealand edition published in 2003 by Hodder Moa Beckett Publishers [a member of the Hodder Headline Group],
4 Whetu Place, Mairangi Bay, Auckland, New Zealand.

Designed by Kylie Nicholls. Printed by Midas Printing Limited, Hong Kong.

www.milkphotos.com

ISBN 0 7336 1804 9

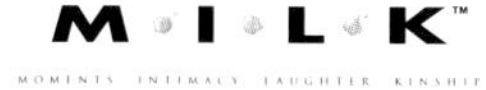

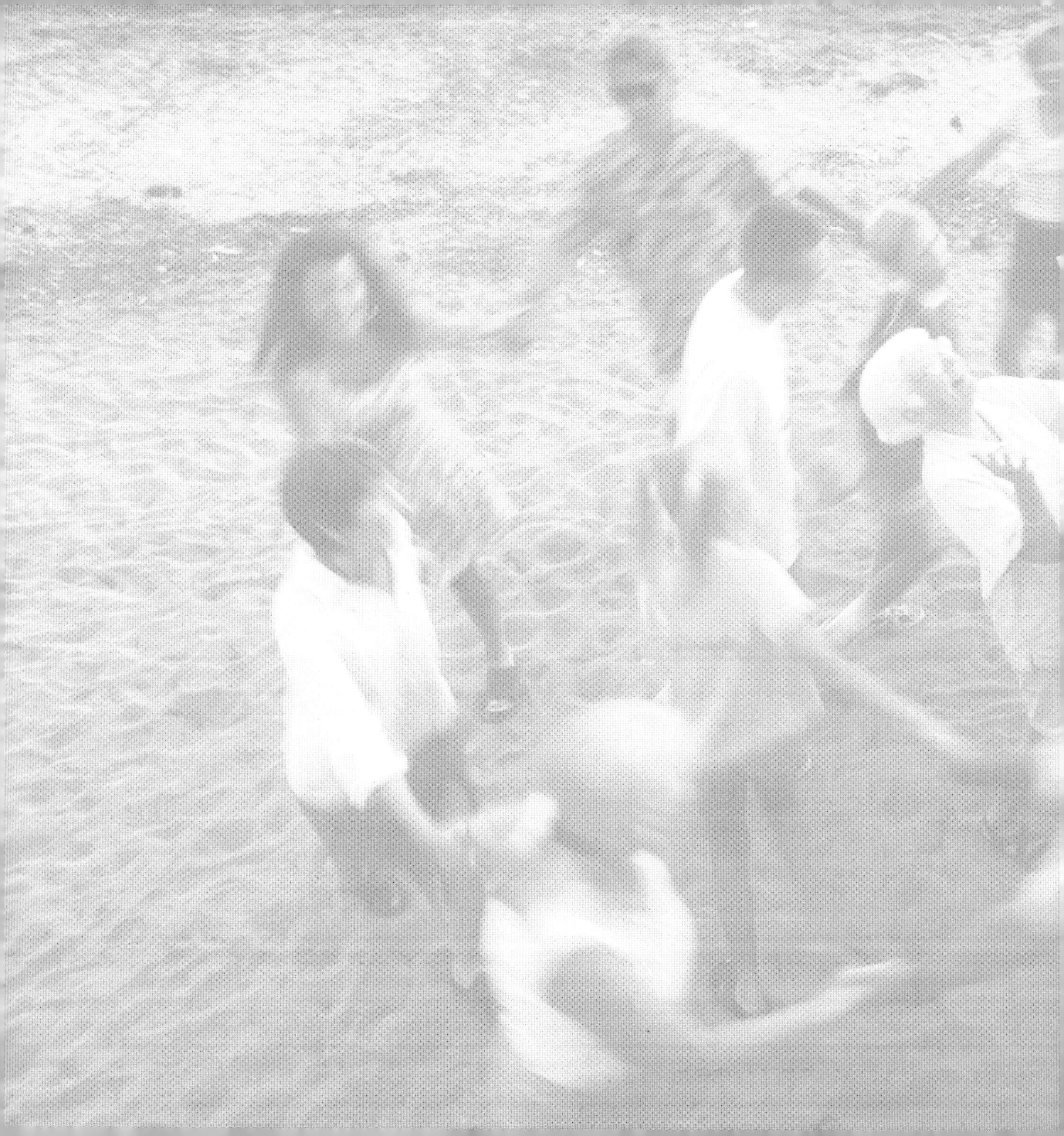